Tall el-Hammam Excavation Project

Tall el-Hammam
Reconstruction of the MB gate
L. Ritmeyer

Field Manual

Steven Collins, Carroll Kobs, Phillip Silvia

The Tall el-Hammam Excavation Project is a Joint Scientific Endeavor between Trinity Southwest University's Department of Archaeology and the Department of Antiquities of the Hashemite Kingdom of Jordan.

Trinity Southwest University Press
Albuquerque, New Mexico

Trinity Southwest University Press
Albuquerque, New Mexico
www.TSUPress.com

The *Tall el-Hammam Excavation Project Field Manual* was created by several staff members of the Tall el-Hammam Excavation Project and Trinity Southwest University under the general guidance of Dr. Steven Collins. Major contributions were provided by Dr. Carroll Kobs and Phillip Silvia.

Library of Congress No: 2013951272
ISBN-13: 978-0615891828
ISBN-10: 0615891829

CREDITS: Front Cover Page Illustration: Leen Ritmeyer, Director of Architectural Design
The underlying satellite ground image on back cover and in Figures 1-3: Google Earth®.
The underlying topographical map in Figures 4-5: Qutaiba Dasougi, Senior Surveyor, Jordan Department of Antiquities
Photos: Michael C. Luddeni, Director of Photography

Tall el-Hammam Excavation Project
Field Manual

Table of Contents

List of Figures

INTRODUCTION

Beyond this *Field Manual* for the Tall el-Hammam Excavation Project (TeHEP), we highly recommend reading *A Complete Manual of Field Archaeology: Tools and Techniques of Field Work for Archaeologists* by Martha Joukowsky (Prentice Hall, 1980, 630 pages).

The primary purpose of this *Field Manual* is to provide TeHEP Square, Field and Area Supervisors with an overview of the tools, techniques and methodologies employed at Tall el-Hammam. Also of major emphasis is data collection and the proper use of the numerous forms that are used to collect the data and accurately document the progress of the Project.

This edition of the *Field Manual* has been updated for Season Ten (2015) and is mandatory reading for all supervisors at the Tall el-Hammam Excavation Project.

PART ONE – General Information

1 GENERAL OVERVIEW

The Tall el-Hammam Excavation Project (TeHEP) is a joint scientific endeavor between Trinity Southwest University, Albuquerque, New Mexico, USA and the Department of Antiquities of the Hashemite Kingdom of Jordan. The goal of TeHEP is to study the relationship of this immense and strategically-located site within its ancient period socio-cultural, economic and political contexts, and to ascertain its position, function and influence within those contexts.

In addition to this broader focus incorporating historical and archaeological data from neighboring sites in the southern Jordan Valley and beyond, the Project is studying the site as a microcosm of life and activity within its own local environment, seeking to determine its phases of settlement, urbanization and the reasons for its decline, destruction and/or abandonment at archaeological period interfaces.

Within this micro-context, the Project seeks to shed light on how the inhabitants of Tall el-Hammam adapted to the local environment and environmental changes, and utilized available resources, enabling them to attain levels of city planning and building on a resultantly large scale, particularly during the Bronze Age.

The present overview seeks to provide a general synopsis of the historical, geographical, chronological, and archaeological data distilled from over a decade of exploration and excavation at, and in the vicinity of, this remarkable site, and to foster interest in Tall el-Hammam as a significant source of present and future information regarding the history of the southern Jordan Valley and, indeed, of the southern Levant.

The civilization occupying the southern end of the Jordan River Valley had maintained a continuous presence that can be traced back to at least the Chalcolithic Period (ca. 4500 BCE). It even survived the great collapse of the climate that ended the Early Bronze (EB) Age (ca. 2350 BCE). While most of the urban centers throughout the Near East collapsed at the beginning of the following Intermediate Bronze (IB) Age and the people adopted a nomadic or semi-nomadic lifestyle, the civilization occupying the urban centers of the southern end of the Jordan River Valley survived and thrived due to the availability of perennial sources of water. During the Middle Bronze (MB) Age, however, the civilization occupying the eastern side of the southern end of the Jordan River Valley seems to have suffered a catastrophic termination ca. 1700 (±50) BCE coinciding with the simultaneous destruction of its principal urban center, Tall el-Hammam. Based on the pottery record from sites that have been excavated in this area, 600-700 years elapsed between their termination and the next significant occupation of the area during the Iron Age, ca. 900 BCE. The Tall Nimrin excavators coined the term "Late Bronze (LB) Gap" to describe the absence of LB pottery at their site, and this term can rightly be applied to the other sites in the area.

Tall el-Hammam (TeH) is located 12.6 km NE of the Dead Sea, 11.7 km E of the Jordan River, 8 km south of the modern village of South Shouna (the location of Tall Nimrin), and approximately 1 km SSW of the Kafrayn Dam. This area of the southern Jordan Valley, particularly the eastern half of what should properly be called "the Jordan Disk"[1] (the circular alluvial area north of the Dead Sea, approximately 25 km in diameter, also called the middle Ghor), lies on the crossroads of the region's ancient N/S and E/W trade routes.[2] Several significant sites, all variously occupied during the high points of Levantine Bronze Age[3] civilization, hug the eastern edge of the Jordan Disk beyond the spread of the ancient flood plain, bounded on the north by the throat of the Jordan Valley, and on the south by the rocky terrain of the Dead Sea area (see Figure 1)—Tall Nimrim with Tall Bleibel and Tall Mustah in close proximity, and sprawling Tall el-Hammam encircled by Tall Tahouna (NE), Tall Barakat (N), Tall Kafrayn (NW), Tall Rama (SW), Tall Mwais (SSW), Tall Iktanu (SSE), and several small un-named sites, all within a .75 to 2.7 km radius of Hammam (Glueck 1945; Ibrahim and Yassine 1988; Khouri 1988; Leonard 1992; Chang-Ho 2002). Although the ancient eastern Jordan Disk towns and villages vary site to site as to periodization, particularly during the Bronze Age, Tall el-Hammam was their connecting common denominator positioned at the center of what must surely be described as a city-state—and a relatively large one at that.

Also nearby are several large dolmen fields (Prag 1995; Aljarrah tbp) and tombs that, to a large extent, remain unexcavated or robbed out,[4] although we have excavated several dolmens and have re-surveyed the area as the Hammam Megalithic Field.[5] The Hellenistic, Roman, and Byzantine periods are represented architecturally at and near the site, including forts, guard towers, aqueducts, large cisterns, and by at least one monumental structure located on the S side of Tall el-Hammam near two springs, one thermal, one sweet.[6] Tall el-Hammam is the largest of the Jordan Disk sites. It is certainly one of the

---

[1] The wide, circular, flat alluvial area of the southern Jordan Valley immediately north of the Dead Sea is approximately 25 km in diameter, and split down the center by the Jordan River. The biblical term for this phenomenologically disk-shaped region is *kikkar* (= disk, circle), appearing as *hakikkar* (the disk/circle) and *kikkar hayarden* (disk/circle of the Jordan River). When not used geographically, *kikkar* refers either to a talent (flat, circular weight of metal) or a flat, circular loaf of bread. Although cognate forms of *kikkar* appear in virtually all ANE languages (including Akkadian, Ugaritic, and Egyptian), the term is never used in a geographical sense outside the Old Testament, but always refers to a disk-like "talent" or "loaf." The rare, geographical usage of *kikkar* lies at the core of the phrases "Plain (*kikkar*) of the Jordan River" and "Cities of the Plain (*kikkar*)" as seen in Genesis 10-19. The entire area was visible from the highland hilltops near the Jordan Valley WNW of Jericho, the location of Bethel and Ai (see Genesis 13:1-12).

[2] There is debate regarding whether or not some kind of traversable road or trail existed on or near the eastern and western shores of the Dead Sea by which travelers could move N and S through the Dead Sea Valley. Even though much of the terrain was difficult, it is hard to believe that at least some kind of stable footpath did not exist, affording one the opportunity to move from towns/sites near the Dead Sea shore northward into the Jordan Valley without having to mount up into the high terrain to connect up with roads on the Trans- and Cisjordan plateaus, then return to the Jordan Valley at a location farther to the N.

[3] See the new archaeological period abbreviations in section, "Stratigraphy" in Collins, Hamdan, Byers, et al 2009a.

[4] The Hammam (ar-Rawda) dolmens tend to be on the higher, flatter parts of the hills to the ESE of Tall el-Hammam, while the tombs are below them in the steeper walls of the wadis. However, there is evidence that at least a few dolmens were located very close to the tall itself, on the adjacent alluvial plain.

[5] K. Schath, S. Collins and H. Aljarrah, "The Excavation of an Undisturbed Demi-Dolmen and Insights from the Ḥammām Megalithic Field, 2011 Season," *Annual of the Department of Antiquities of Jordan* 55 (2011).

[6] Dr. David Graves and Dr. Scott Stripling reason that this must somehow be connected to the ancient Roman city of Livias, perhaps a guesthouse or palatial structure on the eastern edge of the Livias precincts.

largest, if not the largest, Bronze Age site in Jordan. It was the largest city in the southern Levant for much of the Bronze Age.

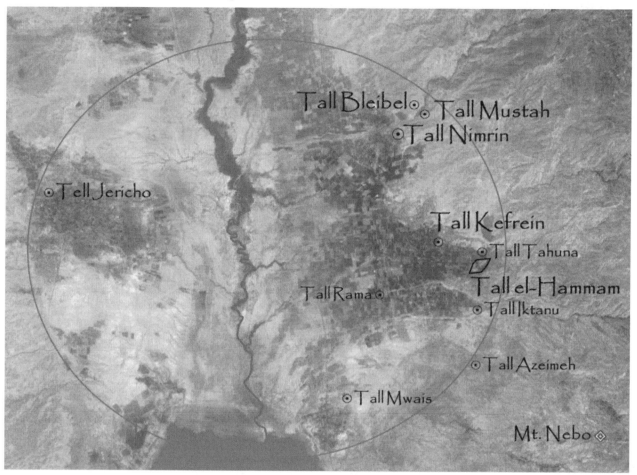

Figure 1 - Significant Sites in the Middle Ghor

The tall proper spreads over approximately 36 ha (360 dunams), bounded by the Wadi Kafrayn on the north and the Wadi Ar Rawda on the south, and by the main road to the E of the tall, against the foothills, and the confluence of these two wadis to the W (see Figure 2).

The Bronze Age fortified footprint is about 26 ha (62 acres). The site footprint for general settlement is well over 400 dunams (100+ acres). These dimensions approximate the areas of the site occupied in more remote antiquity, from at least the Chalcolithic Period through the late Iron Age (with an occupational gap following its MB2 destruction until IA2[7]). There is, additionally, ample evidence of Hellenistic/E Roman/Byz Period occupation just off the upper tall to the immediate south (see Figure 3). Reports about the site from the late 19th

---

[7] For example, the smaller Iron Age occupation, confined to the upper tall, covers approximately 12 ha.

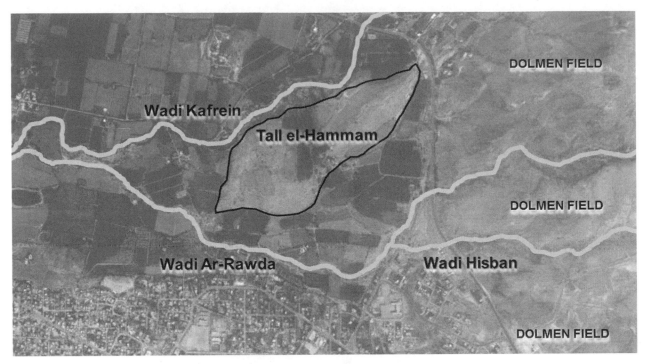

Figure 2 - Tall el-Hammam Vicinity

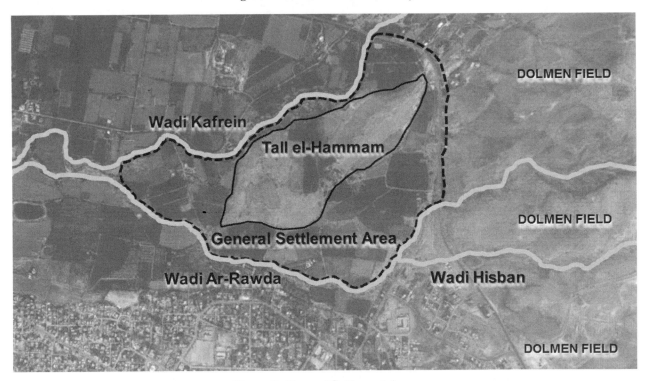

Figure 3 - General Settlement Area

century (Tristram 1874: 330-333; Thomson 1882: 371-376) describe an aqueduct that fed the area south of the upper tall, much of which we have identified. There also seems to have been some re-use of earlier structures on the upper tall (particularly those built initially

8

during the Iron Age) periodically from the Iron Age through the Late Islamic Period. However, sherds from the Islamic Period are rare.

Surface surveying and excavation reveal occupation beginning at least during the Chalcolithic Period (some Neolithic material is also present) and extending with detectable consistency through the Early Bronze Age, the Intermediate Bronze Age, and into the Middle Bronze Age (all with associated architecture). Late Bronze Age sherds seem systematically absent on the site, and there is no discernible LBA[8] architecture (the only possible LBA sherds from around the site were found in a tomb). One of the more surprising discoveries during Season Four and confirmed through Season Eight was that the EBA city wall extended not just around the lower tall (as originally thought), but also around the entire base of the upper tall as well. Equally surprising was the fact that the MBA city fortifications were not confined to the mudbrick/earthen rampart ringing the upper tall (Parr 1968; Burke 2008; McAllister 2008), but also extended around the lower tall. During Season Five, it was discovered that the MBA city wall and rampart system, aggregately from 33m to 50m thick, buried and dwarfed the 6m-thick EBA city wall with its many towers and (likely) multiple gates (Zayadine, Najjar, and Greene 1987; Najjar 1992; Burke 2008; Falconer 2008). Also during previous seasons, detailed surface sherding of the lower tall revealed a large quantity of ceramic forms dating to the Intermediate Bronze Age (cf. Homès-Fredericq and Franken 1986: 98-114; Brown 1991; Palumbo 2008), indicating that the city likely survived the ubiquitous period-ending calamity that caused the demise of EBA cities throughout the Levant, many of which never recovered (Richard 1987; Ben Tor 1992; Finkelstein and Gophna 1993; Harrison 1997; Avner and Carmi 2001; Philip 2008). This was confirmed stratigraphically and architecturally during Seasons Five, Six, Seven and Eight. Perhaps owing to Tall el-Hammam's access to multiple water resources (the Jordan River, seasonal rainfall and wadi flows,[9] and numerous nearby and on-site springs), residents seem to have overcome the negative factors leading to the decline and/or demise of other cities in the region (Prag 2007).[10]

Like Tall el-Hammam, nearby Bronze Age sites such as Tall Nimrin, Tall Iktanu, and Tall Kafrayn[11] (and all others in eastern Jordan Disk area, for that matter) seem to lack discernable, or any, Late Bronze Age occupation (Dornemann 1990; Prag 1974, 1991; Strange 2008). The "LBA gap"—as the Tall Nimrin excavators call it (Flanagan, McCreery, Yassine 1990, 1992, 1994, 1996)—phenomenon seems confined to the Jordan Kikkar, and TeH is shedding light on what may have caused it. Whatever caused the absence of

---

[8] See the new archaeological period abbreviations in section "V. Stratigraphy" in Collins, Hamdan, Byers, et al 2009a.

[9] In antiquity, both the Wadi Kufrayn and the Wadi Ar Rawda/Hisban probably sustained perennial flows more often than not.

[10] Tall Iktanu, 2 km to the S of Tall el-Hammam, also has strong IBA occupation, but not fortified. Although Tall Iktanu has generally been seen as a defining IBA representative in most of the relevant literature, it must now be interpreted as one of many satellites of the much larger, and fortified, Tall el-Hammam.

[11] Although not much has been published on the excavation at Tall Kufrayn, our personal contact with the director of the excavation confirms that there is not an LBA architectural presence at the site. There is a strong EBA and MBA presence, as at Tall Nimrin.

occupation at the eastern Jordan Disk sites during the LBA/IA1 timeframe did, in fact, not continue, as many sites were resettled toward the end of Iron Age 1 into Iron Age 2 (cf. Dornemann 1983). Indeed, the Iron Age 2 occupation at TeH is quite extensive, and surrounded by a 3+m thick fortification wall, perhaps casemate, at least in part. What gave rise to the site's Iron Age city, and what brought about its demise? The answers to these questions are only beginning to be answered.

TeHEP has also produced significant advancements in the area of landscape archaeology and anthropology in terms of the Hammam city-state as a phenomenologically-defined, holistic integration of urbascape, agriscape, sacrescape, necroscape, and infrascape. The inter-relationships between these city-state components is leading us to consider new ideas about socio-cultural-religious-economic aspects of the EBA-IBA-MBA urbanization processes, based on data and observations from Hammam-proper and related research and exploration during intervening off-seasons. New insights on, and interpretations of, the southern Levantine Bronze Age are emerging from this growing body of material.

Tall el-Hammam certainly holds key pieces of the archaeological puzzle from which a greater comprehension and appreciation of the regional history can emerge. Due to the unique topography of Tall el-Hammam, we have divided the tall into two excavation areas, as shown in Figure 4. Our continuing focus is to identify and sound sections of the site determined to offer reasonable opportunities to expose stratigraphic sequencing on the lower tall (Area L) and upper tall (Area U) while, at the same time, continuing to survey, map, and document important geographical features and archaeological sites on the eastern Jordan Disk, with a view to determining the relationship of Tall el-Hammam to the territory under its hegemony and to surrounding polities.

When considering its constituent components collectively, TeH is enormous. Our extensive explorations of the Tall el-Hammam general occupational area during the first six seasons led us to consider its position as a major, fortified city at the hub of a definable Bronze Age city-state, particularly during the EBA through the MBA. However, we have since extended the scope of this research to include not only Tall el-Hammam and its occupational platform between the Wadi Kafrayn and Wadi Ar Rawda, but also its relationship to smaller sites encircling it, particularly to the N, W, and S, all within a radius of 5 km.[12] Therefore, it has remained important for us to continue to survey the locations of outlying talls, dolmens, and tombs in order to flesh out a more comprehensive picture of the socio-political structure existing between Tall el-Hammam and its many satellites.

---

[12] Many of these sites tend to hug the circle of foothills to the S and N, while others occupy positions on the alluvial plain to the SW, W, and NW. Distances from the center of Tall el-Hammam range from .25 km to approximately 5 km. All are within direct line-of-sight from the top of Hammam's upper and lower talls within a visually and geographically defined and defensible space.

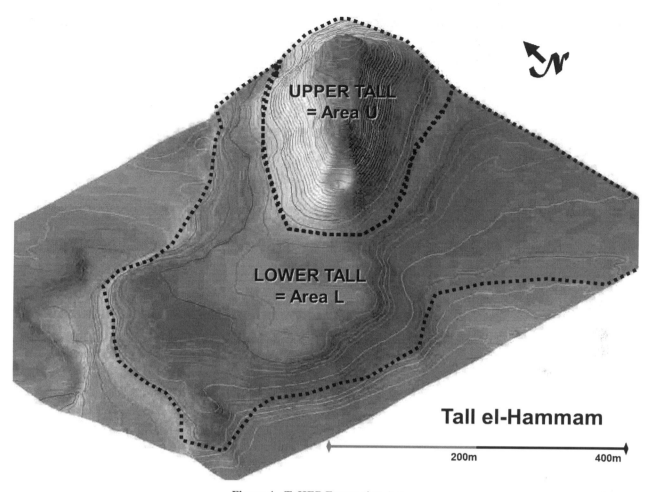

Figure 4 - TeHEP Excavation Areas

The exposure of multi-phase Bronze Age domestic and fortification architecture on lower Hammam has set the stage for furthering our understanding of these features by continuing to expand the number of excavated fields, as shown in Figure 5.

Field LA is adjacent to, and includes, a well-defined section of the Bronze Age city walls and gateways, and includes several domestic structures inside the perimeter defenses. Field A is also a raised area offering the potential of deep stratigraphy, and it has not fallen prey to deep-plowing agricultural activity. Indeed, work in this trench suggests unbroken occupation in the form of Chalcolithic, EB1-2-3, IB1-2, and MB1-2 architectural remains. The eastward expansion of this trench has led to the discovery of a monumental MBA gateway system complete with both small and large defensive towers, and a unique, pillared gatehouse.

Field LB contains large, intact portions of the city's SW defenses, including large towers abutted by thick mudbrick ramparts. One of the towers has already been excavated, revealing a complex structure and history. Additional work in this field is certainly a target.

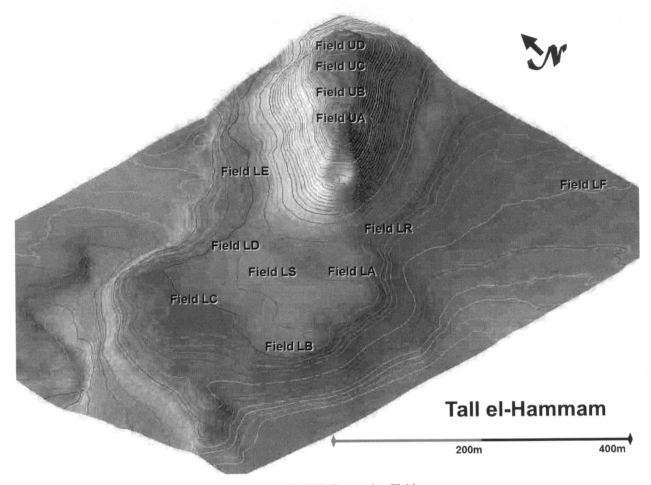

Figure 5 - TeHEP Excavation Fields

Although Field LC contains many surface-visible structures, it has been severely damaged by farming. However, we have excavated part of an IBA house in one sounding. Excavations will continue in this area, and will likely produce significant domestic data.

Field LS is a mixture of Bronze Age administrative and temple-related buildings, with an extramural IA2 structure as well. Remains of a monumental temple structure were unearthed, along with related altars architecture, but military and farming damage to the area is significant for the more surface MB and IA levels. We did detect, and partially excavate, monumental mudbrick EB/IB structures underneath, but that section of Field S has now been covered over and is being farmed again. The W area of Field S is still being excavated.

The large Roman/Byzantine/Islamic structure in Field LR is the central Classical Period feature at the site. Thus, we design to expand upon what has been accomplished there thus far. Several architectural phases are now visible, including baths and associated plumbing.

Field LD is allowing us to 'organically' connect the lower tall with the upper tall. It is revealing a wide range of structures from the Bronze Age and IA2, and contains the lower sections of large retaining walls supporting the approach road to the IA2 gateway (in Field

UB), which roadway also served the gateway of the fortified MB2 upper city. Excavations in Field LE have revealed numerous Iron Age storage silos that were cut into the EDA and MBA rampart walls. Continued excavation of Field LE will provide further information of how the upper and lower cities were connected during the Bronze Age.

On the upper tall, Fields UA, UB, UC, and UD have exposed monumental and domestic Bronze Age and IA2 architecture, including an IA2 gateway and MB2 house (Field UB), a palatial IA2 building and an underlying MB2 palace (?) (Field UA), IA2 houses (Field UC and Field UD). The upper tall is surrounded by IA2 defensive walls and an enormous underlying MBA rampart constructed entirely of mudbricks.

Because archaeological interpretations of excavated data can often be rather two-dimensional, we knew that, for the city-state of Tall el-Hammam, a holistic integration of multiple lines of inquiry was in order. The growing body of field data from surveys, excavations (in the urban center, dolmens, tombs, stone circles and menhir alignments), observations vis-a-vis landscape usage and alteration, and data from surrounding sites requires continued discussion and consideration.

As a result of past and continuing exploration, surveying, and excavation on both upper and lower Tall el-Hammam (along with the nearby Hammam Megalithic Field and tombs), we have assembled adequate data allowing us to continue site-mapping and reconstruction drawings by archaeological architect, Dr. Leen Ritmeyer. We continue to incorporate new stratigraphic and architectural data into our formal site plans, section drawings, and reconstruction drawings for publication purposes.

As is now widely accepted, Tall el-Hammam remains the most logical candidate for biblical Sodom based on a detailed analysis of the relevant biblical and historical materials regarding the chronology and location of the city (Tristram 1874: 330-333; Thomson 1882: 371-376; Collins 2002a, 2002b, 2002c, 2008; cf. MacDonald 2000: 45-61).[13] Extensive research, along with archaeological data from eight seasons of excavation, are now leading many scholars to entertain or adopt this theory on its evidential merits. That the enduring and powerful presence of Tall el-Hammam and its associated towns and villages on the eastern Jordan Disk during the Bronze Age gave rise to the Cities of the Plain tradition reflected in the stories of Genesis 10-19 is a reasonable theory commensurate with all of the available geographical and archaeological data. Future tourism potential for such a site as Tall el-Hammam must not be overlooked or underestimated. From all perspectives, preservation of this highly important site is imperative.

---

[13] See S. Collins and L.C. Scott, *Discovering the City of Sodom* (New York: Howard Books/Simon and Schuster, 2013.

2 STRATIGRAPHY AND RELATED TERMINOLOGY

When no sub-period designations are identified, general references to the archaeological periods use the following abbreviations: Pre-Pottery Neolithic Period = PPNP; Pottery Neolithic Period = PNP; Chalcolithic Period = CP; Early Bronze Age = EBA; Intermediate Bronze Age = IBA; Middle Bronze Age = MBA; Late Bronze Age = LBA; Iron Age = IA; Hellenistic Period = HP; Early Roman Period = ERP; Late Roman Period = LRP; Byzantine Period = BP. Islamic Periods use the traditional designations. We apply the following general chronology (Collins, Hamdan, Byers, et al 2009a), with new abbreviations given first:

PNP	**Pottery Neolithic Period**	**6000-4500 BCE**	
PN1	Pottery Neolithic/early	6000-5500 BCE	
PN2	Pottery Neolithic/middle	5500-5000 BCE	
PN3	Pottery Neolithic/late	5000-4500 BCE	
CP	**Chalcolithic Period**	**4500-3600 BCE**	
CP1	Chalcolithic/early	4500-4100 BCE	
CP2	Chalcolithic/middle	4100-3800 BCE	
CP3	Chalcolithic/late	3800-3500 BCE	
EBA	**Early Bronze Age**	**3500-2350 BCE**	
EB1a	Early Bronze 1/early	3500-3300 BCE	
EB1b	Early Bronze 1/middle	3300-3200 BCE	
EB1c	Early Bronze 1/late	3200-3100 BCE	
EB2a	Early Bronze II/early	3100-3000 BCE	
EB2b	Early Bronze II/middle	3000-2900 BCE	
EB2c	Early Bronze II/late	2900-2800 BCE	
EB3a	Early Bronze III/early	2800-2650 BCE	
EB3b	Early Bronze III/middle	2650-2500 BCE	
EB3c	Early Bronze III/late	2500-2350 BCE	
IBA	**Intermediate Bronze Age**	**2350-1950 BCE**	
IB1	Intermediate Bronze/earlier	2350-2200 BCE	(EB IV)
IB2	Intermediate Bronze/later	2200-1950 BCE	(MB I)
MBA	**Middle Bronze Age**	**1950-1550 BCE**	
MB1	Middle Bronze I	1950-1800 BCE	(MB IIA)
MB2	Middle Bronze II	1800-1550 BCE	(MB IIB-C)
LBA	**Late Bronze Age**	**1550-1200 BCE**	
LB1	Late Bronze I	1550-1400 BCE	
LB2a	Late Bronze IIA	1400-1300 BCE	
LB2b	Late Bronze IIB	1300-1200 BCE	
IA	**Iron Age**	**1200-332 BCE**	
IA1a	Iron Age IA	1200-1100 BCE	
IA1b	Iron Age 1B	1100-1000 BCE	
IA2a	Iron Age IIA	1000-900 BCE	
IA2b	Iron Age IIB	900-700 BCE	
IA2c	Iron Age IIA	700-539 BCE	

IA3	Iron Age III/Persian Period	539-332 BCE
HP	**Hellenistic Period**	**332-63 BCE**
RP	**Roman Period**	**53 BCE-324 CE**
ERP	Early Roman Period	63 BCE-135 CE
LRP	Late Roman Period	135-324 CE
BP1	1st Byzantine Period	324-629 CE
	Persian	614-629 CE
BP2	2nd Byzantine Period	629-638 CE
	1st Moslem	638-1099 CE
	Crusader	1099-1187 CE
	2nd Moslem	1187-1517 CE
	Ottoman Turks	1517-1917 CE
	British Mandate	1917-1948 CE

The stratigraphic profile of Tall el-Hammam had long been suspected, but is now being confirmed by excavation (Prag 1974, 1991; Ibrahim, Yassine, and Sauer 1988). The following is a theoretical stratigraphic profile based on observations from extensive sherding, clearing and clarification of MT disturbances, and the results of scientific excavation through eight seasons. By "theoretical stratigraphy" we mean what is suggested by a "general assessment" of the ceramic indicators over the whole of the site, giving consideration to the frequency of certain period diagnostics. In other words, significant amounts of pottery from a given period would indicate, theoretically, that an architecturally-based occupation would be likely. On the other hand, rare occurrences of ceramics from a given period would suggest, theoretically, the unlikelihood of a substantial architectural complex dating to that timeframe. Of course, only excavation can reveal the *actual* stratigraphic profile of a given location on the site. Ceramic indicators with associated architecture suggest the following occupational sequence at Tall el-Hammam:

Early-to-Late Islamic Periods. These ceramic forms seem to be mixed into contexts with the latest (surface) structures on the upper and lower talls. Re-use of older structures may account for this, especially in the area of the Roman/Byzantine bath complex on the lower tall (Field LR), where Umayyad pottery is fairly common. However, such sherds are extremely rare on the site as compared to Bronze and Iron Age pottery forms. Only an occasional campsite can be extrapolated from these few Islamic sherds.

Late Hellenistic/Early Roman Period and Byzantine Period. The Late Hellenistic and Early Roman periods are represented at the site, but play a minor role in comparison to the Bronze and Iron Age ceramic assemblages. Roman and Byzantine sherds are present, but are mostly found in two isolated locations, Field LR (monumental building) and Field UA (small guard tower).

Iron Age 1, 2, 3. The Iron Age city is quite extensive on the upper tall, but at this point periodization/phasing is not entirely clear. Iron I pottery is infrequent at this point, but present (such as the IA1b pilgrim flask found in Field UB). The IA2b-c monumental gateway in Field UB has an earlier phase dating to IA2a (perhaps late IA1b), with the terminal phase dating to IA2c, perhaps IA3. The principal Iron Age city at Tall el-Hammam seems to have been built during IA2a-b. IA3 (Persian Period) sherds are present-but-infrequent at this point.

Late Bronze Age. Material from the Late Bronze Age is systematically absent from the tall proper. However, LB2 pottery vessels were found in a nearby tomb containing vessels dating from the Chalcolithic Period through the Iron Age. Thus, some kind of LB2 presence in the area can be surmised; however, no architecture from that period is known in this vicinity of the valley E of the Jordan River.

Middle Bronze Age. Both MB1 and MB2 are strongly represented in the TeH ceramic repertoire, typical MBA bronze weaponry, and in related fortification, monumental, and domestic architecture on both the upper and lower talls. That the strongly fortified MBA city spread over most or all the site footprint is now clear.

Intermediate Bronze Age. IB1 and IB2 pottery forms appear with high frequency across the entire site. These occupants also seem to have re-built and re-used many of the previous EB2/EB3 structures including the city fortifications. IBA domestic structures are clearly confined inside the city walls, with relatively clear indications of fortification alterations (such as the blocking of one of the EB2/3 gateways).

Early Bronze Age. The EBA city of Tall el-Hammam is unmistakable and massive. On the basis of excavations, three phases of the EBA city are clearly visible. EB1 houses protrude from under the EB2 city wall foundation and associated outer roadway. The 5.2m-thick EB2 city wall was dramatically strengthened during EB3. The EBA fortification system surrounds both the lower and upper talls (around the base of the upper tall).

Chalcolithic Period. Chalcolithic pottery forms of the Ghassulian variety are found with some frequency, as are various basalt bowl fragments. The lithic artifacts from this period are fairly common. It would be understandable if Chalcolithic residents (perhaps moving from Tuleilat Ghassul?) had come to Tall el-Hammam to take advantage of its abundant water resources. Given the immense size of the EBA city, it is in the realm of possibility that the footprint of an underlying Chalcolithic settlement at TeH might eventually come to light. Chalcolithic architecture (broadhouses) built on bedrock have already appeared underneath EBA structures.

Confirmed Stratigraphy. A Chalcolithic architectural presence is now confirmed at TeH. The EB2 occupants of the site were the original builders of the extensive fortification systems that surround both the upper and lower talls, and these systems were strengthened significantly during EB3 (Mazar 2002; Schaub 2007; Schaub and Chesson 2007). The Intermediate Bronze Age occupants seem to have utilized most or all of the EBA footprint, including the fortifications. Excavation on the lower tall suggests a continuous occupation from the CP through most of MB2. The Middle Bronze Age is strongly attested architecturally at TeH, particularly in its fortification ramparts and walls on both the upper and lower talls, the monumental gateway on the south side of the lower tall, and in numerous domestic contexts. No structures belonging to the Late Bronze Age or Iron Age 1a are presently known. Perhaps one structure in Field UB can be dated to IA1b, but that identification still needs more study. The IA2 city is extensively attested by both monumental and defensive architecture, and in domestic contexts. Iron 3 seems present, but yet unconfirmed by anything more than re-use of older buildings. Hellenistic, Roman, and Byzantine architecture (re-used?) seem confirmed on the south side of the site, and perhaps in Field UA on the upper tall. Islamic structures are presently unknown, except (perhaps) some minimal re-use of earlier architecture.

3   METHODOLOGICAL INSIGHTS

Based on our stratigraphic analysis of Tall el-Hammam, we offer the following observations and insights in light of the 'traditional' interpretive criteria generally applied in S. Levantine archaeology (such as the Wheeler/Kenyon approach).[14]

Conventional excavation/interpretation is based on what may be called BDA (building-destruction-abandonment) sequencing. Of course, such sequences do exist, giving rise to relatively clear cultural horizons in site strata, accompanied by discreet ceramic assemblages easily separable from earlier and later materials. However, we now suspect that the evolution of BDA interpretive criteria (a la Petrie, Garstang, Albright, Wheeler, Kenyon, and so forth) has perhaps been responsible for some (even serious) misinterpretations of archaeological data due to its generally two-dimensional nature. A. Rainey wisely noted that sites are three-dimensional in nature and must be interpreted in this manner (Rainey and Notley 2006: 23ff).

A BDA sequence is one thing. But what if a site was continuously occupied for a millennium or more, wherein the architectural structures—domestic, monumental, and defensive—were used, re-used, re-furbished, and expanded over an extremely long period of time? In such a continuous-occupation scenario, not only would the local culture be more monolithic and resistant to change from 'outsiders', but also the evolution of the material culture over time would lend itself to 'blurred', generally indistinct horizons; indeed, separability might be virtually absent in many locations around a given site.

By way of an example, consider that a house was originally built during the EB3 period, but was continuously occupied (in whole or in part, depending on its structural integrity over time) through the IBA and MBA. Rooms and upper floors may be added during later periods (continuously, in an evolutionary fashion), and older sections of the same house may be re-plastered, re-floored, or re-buttressed during subsequent times. Certain lower/older rooms may continue to be used, or might be filled in with debris for structural reasons. Some upper stories may be later or earlier in construction than other parts of the building, and some lower ones may also be earlier or later as the structure(s) evolve bit-by-bit in response to accidental fires, natural (annual) deterioration (typical of mudbrick construction), earthquakes, replacement of rotting roof beams, renewal of floor plasters, the addition of storage and living space, etc., over extended periods of time.

Several centuries of such continuity spanning conventional archeological horizons would be very difficult, if not impossible to detect and interpret using traditional BDA sequence criteria. Indeed, the ceramics embedded in now-collapsed and compacted debris might 'favor' the EB3 lower down and the MB2 higher up, but there would be no clear ceramic horizon, only a trend-driven graduality as forms from outside the city's enduring core culture managed to penetrate into the local ceramic repertoire 'guarded' by long-standing morphological conventions inextricably bound up with the socio- religio-complexities of a tribal, clan-based urban culture (example: Tall el-Hammam's millennia-enduring

---

[14] Based on the research and analysis of TeHEP Chief Archaeologist, S. Collins.

holemouth jar and cooking pot tradition that began in the late CP and lasted into the MBA, resisting the integration of the more open forms such as the MBA rounded-bottom cooking pots and straight-sided 'casseroles' typically found in Cisjordan repertoires).

In terms of ethnographic analogues, there are many. The Native American pueblos of New Mexico, also built of mudbrick, are a prime example. Many of these mudbrick 'towns' have been continuously occupied for hundreds, even a thousand or more years, with the oldest (certainly repaired/modified) structures integrated with the most recent ones, and everything in between. In these contexts, heirloom ceramics endure in use (fast potter's wheels are still resisted today!), and contemporary forms preserve ancient traditions and artistic motifs often with great fidelity. These 'cities'—such as Taos Pueblo, which has been continuously occupied for the past 1,200 years—are comparable in size with Levantine Bronze Age sites. They constitute living, organic complexes of architectural evolution without a 'traditional' stratigraphic character in the generally-understood ANE sense. Indeed, at Taos, residents continue to maintain, refurbish, and dwell in houses with foundations, walls, and floors spanning the pueblo's 1,200-year history.[15]

Such an enduring city, when approached by the archaeologist after millennia of abandonment subsequent to its many centuries of continuous occupation—perhaps followed by one or more BDA sequences—would, minimally, be extremely difficult to interpret via the traditional stratigraphic concepts of BDA-based analysis. In such a context, there may very well be MB2 material sitting directly on an EB3 floor. There may be an IBA floor added into an EB3 room with MB1 sherds on that floor. There may be an MB2 installation built on/into an IBA floor and sealing up against an EB3 mudbrick wall plastered over (again) during MB1. These are only a few scenarios that obtain from a continuously occupied, architecturally-evolving site, not to mention all of the socio-cultural dynamics that would have attended such instances.

These are exactly the kinds of phenomena we are observing on the lower city at Tall el-Hammam. In several places it is possible to trace the evolution of the same basic domestic structure from its EB3 foundations, IBA rebuilds/additions, and MB1/2 refurbishments and additions, all following the same basic footprint and wall-lines, producing a dramatic three-dimensional record of architectural evolution spreading not only horizontally, but also vertically.

There is no rational means of interpreting such complex phenomena when relying on BDA-based methods alone.

Therefore, we are suggesting the development of a new interpretive methodology with (at this point) four main categories of stratigraphic sequencing criteria (we thought it prudent to document some of our thinking in this regard while the data from the most recent seasons are still fresh in our minds):

---

[15] Co-author, S. Collins, is intimately familiar with Taos Pueblo and has personally examined the site on numerous occasions. His background in Southwest Native American ethnology has been extremely beneficial in helping to interpret the occupational patterns at Tall el-Hammam.

Building-Destruction-Abandonment (BDA) Sequence. An enumerative explanation of predictive, observable phenomena (criteria) resulting from a BDA sequence (we will not burden the reader with the details here, but one will see the pattern).

Continuous-Occupation-Expansion (COE) Sequence. An enumerative explanation of predictive, observable phenomena (criteria) resulting from a COE sequence, i.e., a site that is continuously occupied and growing architecturally, with no intervening BDA sequences.

Continuous-Occupation-Maintenance (COM) Sequence. An enumerative explanation of predictive, observable phenomena (criteria) resulting from a COM sequence, i.e., a site that is continuously occupied and maintaining an architectural status quo, with no intervening BDA sequences.

Continuous-Occupation-Reduction (COR) Sequence. An enumerative explanation of predictive, observable phenomena (criteria) resulting from a COR sequence, i.e., a site that is continuously occupied but diminishing architecturally, with no intervening BDA sequence in some locations, but with a BDA sequence(s) in other locations.

One must also consider potential ephemeral (tents? squatting?) occupation, erosion, period site alteration/destruction, modern farming and military activities, and host of other factors.

What we hope to accomplish through this is a rational, logical means of assessing architectural, artifactual, and depositional data (with an attending excavation methodology) that is sensitive to both BDA and continuous-occupation sequences and their attending phenomena (criteria).

Based on some recent examination of excavation reports and even final publications, we detect what is perhaps a degree of potential misinterpretation of data in terms of alleged site abandonments and even alleged site continuation. Perhaps this kind of approach will free some from the straightjacket of previous methods of stratigraphic analysis, allowing a clearer assessment of what, heretofore, had been virtually un-interpretable. Indeed, the concept of a 'sealed' locus would only be categorically applicable in a BDA or COR context, whereas the stratigraphy of a COE or COM sequence would manifest itself in the temporal evolution of at least some components of a site's architectural repertoire (this would be particularly true of domestic architecture, and perhaps less true as a generalization in terms of monumental and defensive architecture).

4   LANDSCAPE ARCHAEO-ANTHROPOLOGY

That Tall el-Hammam was the political and cultural epicenter of a significant Bronze Age city-state is, by now, quite obvious. One can easily comprehend the ancient phenomenological interpretation of the definable and defensible landscape visible from Tall el-Hammam when standing at almost any location on the site. Field UA (location of the MBA palace) provides a particularly dramatic vantage point from which to view the territory under TeH's control (the most logical candidate for the formulaic geography of the Cities of the Plain in biblical lore). In order to make sense of the interwoven complexities of such a socio-political entity, a holistic, integrative approach to the archaeology and anthropology of the area is required.

For purposes of studying the interrelated features of the city-state—such as its central city, outlying towns, villages, and hamlets, agricultural fields, dolmen/menhir fields and tombs—we propose a theoretical structuring of city-state components in terms of landscape utilization based on the readily observable (obvious) partitioning of the local geography by its ancient inhabitants. Since it is clear that the citizens of the TeH city-state incorporated virtually every square kilometer (indeed, square meter) of their landscape environment, the terminology we are suggesting seeks to describe the purposes for which they utilized, augmented, and altered the local terrain. For the TeH city-state in particular, we have (thus far) organized it into five principal macro-features: *urbascape*, *agriscape*, *sacrescape*, *necroscape*, and *infrascape*.[16]

Urbascape: that portion of the landscape utilized, augmented, and altered by the principal population of a city-state incorporating political, religious, administrative, economic, domestic, and defensive architecture, the perimeter of which is defined by fortifications, the aggregate of which is phenomenologically defined by the city-state's inhabitants as the 'core' of their 'kingdom'.

Agriscape: that portion of the landscape utilized, augmented, and altered by the collective agricultural enterprises of the city-state for fields and groves, water management, housing laborers, processing installations, storage and distribution facilities, and the handling of traded agricultural commodities, including interspersed towns (perhaps fortified), villages, and hamlets inhabited by farmers, workmen, and their families.

Sacrescape: that portion of the landscape utilized, augmented, and altered by the collective religious/ritual practices of the city-state community, including many or all of the following components: sacred architecture (such as temples and ritual enclosures), ritual monuments (such as menhirs, stone circles, megalithic alignments, and dolmens), sacred places (such as hilltops, groves, and other topographical features of ritual significance), the necroscape, and the processional thoroughfares by which they are connected and accessed.

Necroscape: that portion of the landscape utilized, augmented, and altered by the collective funerary activities of the city-state community, where the dead are treated,

---

[16] This is the terminology developed by S. Collins, TeHEP Director. This section is based on the research and analysis of S. Collins and L. Clayton, TeHEP Senior Anthropologist in collaboration.

tended, buried, and memorialized, including tombs and monuments of all types devoted to the passage, remembrance, or worship of ancestors, such as cave and shaft tombs, dolmens (various types), menhirs (+ alignments), stone circles, and ritual avenues.

Infrascape: that portion of the landscape utilized, augmented, and altered by the collective activities of the city-state population in support of building and maintenance activities, transportation needs, refuse/sanitation management, and various industries, including stone, earth, and clay quarry sites, roadways, production facilities for mudbricks, ceramics, metallurgy, stone-work, wood-work and other materials.

Each of these macro-components of the TeH city-state has a distinct, visual impact on the observer. These are the 'larger-than-life' physical manifestations of city-state life which incorporate, overlay, and sculpt the landscape via the human enterprise of surviving and thriving within a local environment. As the Tall el-Hammam Excavation Project continues through the present and next decade, it will provide a wealth of data and insights for understanding Bronze Age civilization at the city-state level in the southern Jordan Valley.

5   OPERATIONAL ORGANIZATION

5.1   Staff

The Tall el-Hammam Excavation Project (TeHEP) relies on a variety of Staff and Volunteers to complete its work. Staff is unpaid except for a few specialists.

<u>Executive Staff:</u>
Excavation Director – Steven Collins
Associate Director – Representative from the Jordanian Department of Antiquities
Assistant Excavation Directors – Gary Byers and Carroll Kobs

<u>Senior Staff:</u>
Director of Architectural Reconstruction – Leen Ritmeyer
Director of Photography – Mike Luddeni
Director of Media – Daniel Galassini
Personnel Coordinator – Jean Luddeni
Area Supervisors

<u>Field Staff:</u>
Field Supervisors
Square Supervisors
Surveyors

<u>Support Staff:</u>
Analysis Team & Field Specialists
Pottery Registrar

5.2   Volunteers

Volunteers include all participants accepted to the Project as well as the paid local workers.

If Volunteers have a conflict, they will see their Square Supervisor.
If they have a conflict with their Square Supervisor or a more important matter, they will see the Assistant Excavation Directors.
* * *
If Square Supervisors have concerns regarding their assigned Volunteers, please see the Assistant Excavation Directors.

PART TWO – Field Methods and Data Collection

6   TOOLS, CASES, & SUPPLIES

6.1   Tools

Each Square Supervisor will be assigned a canvas tool bag for his/her Square(s). In it will be trowels, patiches, brushes, and dustpans. Please tell your assigned Volunteers to use only your bag's tools and return them to your bag at the end of each workday. Personal items should not be stored in these bags. Turreahs, Guffahs, Pickaxes, Pottery Buckets, Screens, Tables, Stools, and Wheelbarrows should be divided evenly at the site. One survey bag will be available on site with a large meter tape, survey stakes, balk string, and spray paint (to indicate bench marks).

Figure 6 - Trowels, Patiche and Turreah

Our tools are stored on the site in a locked storage room. All Volunteers and Staff should assist in the loading and unloading of the tools on the truck both at the storage room and at the site location.

6.2   Cases

Each Square Supervisor will be assigned a metal case. Included is: 7.5 m tape measure, string level, 2 small brushes, pen, marker, pencil, rulers, clip board, paperclips, plumb bob, scissors, small baggies for samples, a trowel and a patiche. The case and contents are each Supervisor's responsibility. **The case must be returned with all the contents intact and cleaned out.** Leave the case in the pottery room when you leave Jordan.

6.2.1   Paperwork & Tags

Square Supervisors will need to collect all forms (Locus sheets and additional forms) from the pottery room, as needed. In addition, you are responsible for getting your own pottery and identification tags from the pottery room. The *pottery tags* will go on the pottery buckets. All other artifacts will be tagged using an *identification tag*. At the end of your stay, all tags and paperwork should be removed from your case and placed back in the pottery room. **Give your completed paperwork to Carroll Kobs.** Under no circumstance will you be allowed to take your original paperwork home. (You must get permission from Dr. Collins to take copies of your paperwork home to assist you in writing your end-of-season report.)

6.2.2 Supplies to Bring

Some of the Supervisors have personal copies of the Munsell Soil Color book on the site. These books are expensive and should be treated with care if borrowed and returned immediately after use. Since recording Munsell Color readings is a required step on most Locus forms, you should consider purchasing and bringing your own Munsell book.

At a minimum, Supervisors should bring extra pens, markers, mechanical pencils, and lead. It is also a good idea to bring your own large roll of balk string (mason line) as the site is very large and your Square may be in a different area from the survey bag. The balk string is best if it is colored and slightly stretchy.

Other supplies that Supervisors might consider bringing for personal use include:

- A good (e.g., "Magic Rub") eraser, an erasing shield, and a 6-inch ruler (all very handy for doing your drawings)

- A mechanical pencil (0.5 mm or 0.7 mm) and extra lead

- Extra "Sharpie" markers (black; both fine-point and ultra-fine-point)

- Wide-mouth "Mason" jar lids (drive the bench mark stake through the lid, white side up, and write the bench mark level on the lid with a Sharpie)

- A pocket calculator (unless you are good at doing arithmetic with negative numbers in your head)

- A personal camera for taking lots of pictures of your Volunteers at work in your Squares

- A pocket knife for cutting the balk string

- A small or pocket-size notebook for taking lots of notes (not to be used as a substitute for the forms, but to record names & addresses of Volunteers working in your Squares, writing reminder-notes to self, recording a diary of pictures taken, etc.)

6.2.3 Staff Cell Phones

All Square Supervisors and other Staff members will be given a cell phone for their duration for local calls between Staff Members. Long distance calls are prohibited from these phones. Please make sure your phone is always on and fully charged. When you depart, place the phone and charger in its original box and leave in the pottery room.

7   STAFF MEETINGS & REQUIREMENTS

7.1   Required Staff Meeting

Once each week during the excavation season there will be a required Staff Meeting at a time and place specified by Senior Staff. This will be an informal time to share any insights, problems, or concerns regarding your Square, paperwork, or excavation related events during the midweek. This will allow everyone to hear the overall progress in all Areas and Fields.

7.2   Additional Requirements

All Staff and Volunteers are expected to be present for a "Welcome & Introductions" meeting after breakfast on Sundays (location to be announced each Season). This is when the new arrivals are assigned to their Squares. For first-time Volunteers, there will be a site orientation at the site that same morning.

All Staff members are expected to ride the bus each workday. There will be a staff car that will be used for special assignments and to carry breakable and valuable media and photo equipment. On days off, this car may be shared by all Staff.

8   GENERAL GUIDELINES

The following guidelines apply to all Staff:

1. As a Staff member, you represent the Tall el-Hammam Project and Trinity Southwest University to all Volunteers and Jordanians.

2. Be respectful and positive towards our Project, Goals, and fellow Staff members.

3. Volunteers will have received the Volunteer Manual and should be familiar with our basic methodology, but they will need personal instruction and training in the field.

4. A Jordanian Staff member will assign local workers to Square Supervisors. These local workers are to bring their own water. Many smoke and need to be reminded that cigarettes are only allowed outside the Square area. They are only to be paid by Dr. Collins on the set payday, so no tipping is allowed.

5. The Jordanian workers are hired to assist with the heavy lifting and other tasks. Treat them with respect as you would any Volunteer.

6. Only a select few of the Jordanian workers have been certified by Dr. Collins as qualified excavators. Check with him if you have questions.

7. Offer frequent water breaks to all your Volunteers.

8. All Square Supervisors are encouraged to attend the Pottery Reading activities to record your data. Bring your Pottery Reading Summary form, Locus forms, and a pen or pencil to the Reading.

9. Be mindful of all time constraints both on and off the site.

10. There is a Media Policy at Tall el-Hammam – No Facebook, YouTube, Twitter, or other social networking is allowed regarding excavation related finds unless authorized by Dr. Collins. No publications regarding the excavation are allowed without his approval.

9 GENERAL METHODOLOGY

The Tall el-Hammam Excavation Project uses the excavation protocol applied to most excavations in Jordan. The systematic recording and collection of data is designed to support a detailed analysis of the overall site and facilitate the most efficient use of resources. The process of excavating in layers to fully monitor each stratum and identify all various types of Loci is known as the Wheeler-Kenyon Method. This is the methodology used at Tall el-Hammam as it yields the best scientific approach regarding the strata.

After several seasons of excavation, however, we realized that this methodology fell short at Tall el-Hammam. It was slightly inadequate for a thorough and comprehensive analysis because of the complexity due to our long span of continuous occupation. Therefore, we have adapted the Wheeler-Kenyon Method to the unique conditions found at Tall el-Hammam, including creation of our own unique data collection forms.

10 FIELD METHODS

Archaeology is the reconstruction of past human cultures through the study of their material remains as excavated in their stratigraphic contexts. Archaeology, therefore, contains three phases:

1) Data Collection—the excavation of the material remains of past human cultures in their stratigraphic contexts.

2) Analysis—the study of those material remains.

3) Modeling—the reconstruction of past human cultures.

Our primary focus <u>in the field</u> at Tall el-Hammam is the first phase—data collection through excavation. All of our data collection takes place within the context of a Square; therefore, it is essential that the Square Supervisor know how to lay out a square, how to properly open a Square the first time, and how to reopen a Square in a subsequent Season.

10.1 Basic Steps to Laying a Square

At Tall el-Hammam, each Square is 6x6 m. We leave a 1 m. balk on the north and a 1 m. balk on the east. Therefore, the actual excavation takes place in a 5x5 m area. The balks allow a good vertical section view of the Square's strata. At times, you will be instructed by an Area Supervisor or Executive Staff Member to remove one or both of these balks.

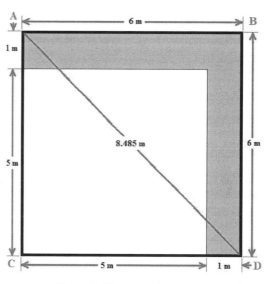

Figure 7 - Laying a Square

Squares are laid out following the overall grid pattern of the site. Preferably, the site Surveyor will stake out each Square. However, since our site is large and the surveyor is in high demand, it is not always possible to acquire the services of the surveyor, and the Square Supervisor may have to lay out a new Square. Note, however, that a Square Supervisor may only lay out a new Square that is contiguous to at least one existing Square.

It takes three people, a 7.5 m measuring tape, and a 10 m measuring tape to lay out a new Square. Referring to the diagram in Figure 7, begin by identifying the two corners of the existing Square that mark the common side of the new Square. Assume for this illustration that the two corners are identified as **A** and **B** in Figure 7, which means that the existing Square is above the illustration. Follow the steps below to locate corners **C** and **D**.

1) To locate corner **D**…

   a) Have the first person hold the loose end of a 10 m measuring tape at corner **A**.

   b) Have the second person hold the loose end of a 7.5 m measuring tape at corner **B**.

c) The third person (the Square Supervisor) should then take the two measuring tapes to the approximate location of corner **D**. Cross the two tapes and adjust your position until the 7.5 m tape reads <u>6.0 m</u> and the 10 m tape reads <u>8.485 m</u> where they cross and both tapes are taut and level.

d) Drive a stake a few cm into the ground directly below the crossing point of the two measuring tapes.

Note: It is important that the tapes be level and held tightly for the measurements to be accurate. If necessary because of sloping ground, use one or more plumb bobs ensure that the ends and crossing point of the tapes are directly over the points on the ground.

2) To locate corner **C**...

a) Have the other two persons change position while you walk over to the approximate location of corner **C**.

b) Repeat steps 1c) and 1d) above for corner **C**.

3) Cross-check your spotting of corners **C** and **D** by measuring the distance between them, which should be <u>6.0 m</u>. If this measurement is off by more than 1 cm (the approximate diameter of the rebar stake), then repeat steps 1) and 2) until you achieve the 1 cm accuracy.

10.2 Basic Steps to Opening a Square

Although the Square is 6 x 6 m, we excavate only a 5 x 5 m area, leaving a 1 m wide balk on the north and east sides of the square. It is up to the Square Supervisor and Volunteers to tie taut strings between the stakes to outline the area of the Square to be excavated.

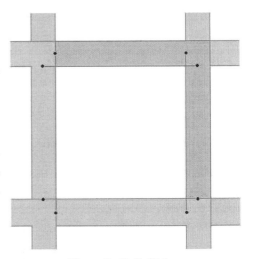

Referring to Figure 8, outline the area to be excavated by driving stakes (black dots) into the middle of the balks surrounding the area, being careful to maintain the lines of the Square. (If balks do not yet exist on one or more sides of the Square, then place the stakes 50 cm from the corners of the area to be excavated.) The crossing points of the string (red lines) mark the corners. Notice that the bottom (in Figure 8) string marks the south side of the Square, and the left string marks the west side of the Square. The top string is parallel to and 1 m south of the north side of the Square, and the right string is parallel to and 1 m west of the east side of the Square.

Figure 8 - Balk Strings

After outlining the area to be excavated with string, add a row of rocks just outside of the strings to remind your Volunteers that they should not step on the edge of a balk. Also, instruct them to always leave all unused tools and personal items outside the working Square.

Next, locate the nearest Bench Mark within your Square's immediate area and use the Bench Mark Form (see Section 4.12, below) to record its relative placement and level. The Surveyor will use a theodolite (total station) to determine the level at least one ("primary") Bench Mark in your area. As our site is below Sea Level, it will be a negative number. If the primary Bench Mark is more than one Square away, use (and record on the Bench Mark Form) one of the string stakes as a "secondary" Bench Mark, and use the Level Calculation Form (see Section 4.13) to determine its level.

Next, Volunteers should remove any debris by hand (no tools) such as loose stones, sticks, leaves, or trash. Cut any rooted plants flush with the surface, but do not pull them up because doing so may disturb artifacts entangled in the roots. Sweep the surface with soft brushes to prepare it for the initial photograph by the Excavation Photographer.

While the volunteers are cleaning the Square, prepare the initial paperwork. At a minimum you will need: a Locus Log form, at least one Soil Locus Form (if the Square is bisected by a visible wall or other feature, then you will need an additional Soil Locus Form and an Architectural Locus Form as well), a Pottery Reading Summary form, and one Pottery Tag for each Locus.

Now your Square is ready for excavation. Fill out a pottery tag and attach it to a pottery bucket (tie it to the handle with a bow, as you would a shoe lace). This will be Locus #1, so start a Soil Locus Form (see Section 4.5). Take opening level readings and record them on your Soil Locus #1 Form.

> *Note: At Tall el-Hammam this first Locus of a Square is the top 5 cm and is considered surface soil. Even though it is considered contaminated, it is still labeled as Locus # 1.*

Volunteers should now be instructed to clear the entire Square to a depth of 5 cm, following the contours of the ground. Take and record closing levels for Locus #1. Next, have Volunteers sweep the Square clean and call the Excavation Photographer for a Locus #1 top photo.

> *Note: Removal of the surface Locus is a good opportunity for you to teach proper troweling technique to new Volunteers since there is usually little risk of encountering or mishandling artifacts in this Locus.*

The Square is now ready for the true excavation process utilizing all the appropriate forms and Top Plan drawings for future Loci (see Section 4, below).

> *Note: Whereas removal of the surface locus follows the contour of the land, the proper technique for the excavation of all analytical soil loci below the surface locus is to start at the highest point and remove the soil in a level manner, as if draining water from a bath tub. Each soil locus should be completely removed, followed by the taking of level readings, before beginning excavation of the next underlying locus.*

10.3 Re-Opening a Square

Study the existing paperwork for the Square. Prepare new Locus Log and Pottery Reading Summary forms (see Section 4) for the current Season, entering the <u>next</u> sequential Locus number and pottery bucket number accordingly as your starting points. Familiarize yourself with the last top plan drawn for the Square so that you will recognize features within the Square as you and your Volunteers clean it.

Re-establish the boundaries and balks for the Square. Attempt to locate the previous Bench Mark(s) used. Have the Surveyor confirm the Bench Mark level or re-establish a new Bench Mark and add the new elevation on the original form.

Clean the Square to remove inter-season debris, including any blown-in or washed-in sand and dirt to locate recognizable features shown in the final top drawing from the previous Season. **This inter-season debris is NOT given a Locus number as it is contaminated, but use an appropriately marked Soil Locus Form to document the clean-up.** If sherds are found in the clean-up soil (usually happens only if inter-season rain was heavy enough to collapse a balk), then assign a Locus number to the clean-up and prepare a Pottery Tag for a bucket to collect the sherds.

11 USING THE DATA COLLECTION FORMS

There is one absolute truth in field archaeology that drives everything we do. That truth is: Through excavation, archaeologists destroy the very site they are researching.   This happens because, once soil and artifacts are removed from the ground, they cannot be replaced. As a result, all data possible must be gleaned from the excavated materials and recorded. There is no second chance! Archaeologists, therefore, must maintain total **control** over every aspect of fieldwork from excavation to record keeping.

Data collection and record keeping are the primary role of a Square Supervisor. Because archaeology is destructive, we rely on specific procedures to accomplish these goals. After using forms from other excavations for the first several seasons, we have developed and implemented our own forms for the Tall el-Hammam Excavation Project. **These forms are a checklist for Supervisors to gather the necessary data needed for later analysis and should be filled out completely.**

Your forms and drawings will be the "eyes" of the Executive Staff when interpreting and recreating the strata and culture at our site during the "off season." All of the forms used at Tall el-Hammam are contained in Appendix A. In summary, the twelve forms are:

1) <u>Forms pertaining to Squares</u>. These forms are required for all Squares and should be included in the Square documentation that you submit when the Square is closed or at the end of the Season, whichever comes first.

   a) Locus Log **[LL]** (see Section 11.2)

   b) Bench Mark Information **[BMI]** (see Section 11.3)

   c) Pottery Reading Summary **[PR]** (see Section 11.4)

   d) Weekly Supervisor Log **[WS]** (see Section 11.5)

2) <u>Forms pertaining to Loci</u>. These forms are required for all Loci that you encounter within a Square and should be included in the Square documentation that you submit when the Square is closed or at the end of the Season, whichever comes first. Not all of these forms will be required in every Square. Use the forms that are appropriate for each type of Locus encountered.

   a) Soil Locus Form **[SL]** (see Section 11.6)

   b) Architectural Locus Form **[AL]** (see Section 11.7)

   c) Functional Surface Locus Form **[FSL]** (see Section 11.8)

   d) Installation Locus Form **[IL]** (see Section 11.9)

   e) Skeleton/Burial Locus Form **[S/BL]** (see Section 11.10)

   f) Identification Tag (see Section 11.11)

   g) Pottery Tag (see Section 11.12)

3) <u>Miscellaneous Forms</u>. These forms are not considered part of the official Square documentation.

  a) Pottery Reading Record **[PR²]** (see Section 11.13)

  b) Level Calculation Form **[LC]** (see Section 11.14)

Detailed instructions for using these forms are presented in the sections that follow.

11.1 General Instructions for Common Form Data

All of the Square and Locus forms contain headers on the front and back to identify the Square and the Locus (on the Locus forms only). Always completely fill out all of the Identification data at the top of the forms, **both front and back.** The Square Identification data block on the front of the forms is shown in Figure 9, the Locus Identification data block on the front of the forms is shown in Figure 10, and the identification data block on the back of the forms is shown in Figure 11 (without the **Locus** # on the Square forms).

SQUARE IDENTIFICATION:				
Season	Square Code (Area/Field/Square)	Date Square Opened (ddmmmyy)	Date Square Closed (ddmmmyy)	Supervisor

Figure 9 - Square Identification Data (Front of Square Forms)

LOCUS IDENTIFICATION:					
Season	Square Code (Area/Field/Square)	Locus #	Date Opened (ddmmmyy)	Date Closed (ddmmmyy)	Supervisor

Figure 10 - Locus Identification Data (Front of Locus Forms)

Season	Square Code	Locus #

Figure 11 - Locus Identification Data (Back of Forms)

The Locus Identification data includes:

☐ **Season** — Enter the entire 4-digit year(s) that the Season covers.
Example: 2013 or 2013-2014 (if more than one calendar year).

☐ **Square Code** — Enter the Area, Field, and Square. Tall el-Hammam has two areas: "U" for Upper Tall, and "L" for Lower Tall. The Field is specific to that Area. The square contains both the north/south coordinate (a number) and east/west coordinate (a letter) of the square's southwest corner.
Example of a Square Code: LA28K means "Lower" Tall, Field "A", and 28K are the coordinates of the Square's southwest corner.

☐ **Locus #** — Enter the Locus number, which is derived from the Locus Log form (see Section 11.2).

☐ **Dates** — Always use the format: *ddmmmyy*, where *dd* is the 2-digit calendar day (include the leading zero for days less than 10); *mmm* in the first three letters of the calendar month (all CAP's); and *yy* is the 2-digit year.
Example: 21JAN13 represents January 21, 2013.

☐ **Supervisor's Names** — Enter the Square Supervisor's first initial and last name.

The data entered into the forms pertaining to Squares (Locus Log, Pottery Reading Summary, and Weekly Supervisor Log) and the miscellaneous forms (Bench Mark and Level Calculation) may span more than one copy the form; thus, they contain a sheet number block as shown in Figure 12.

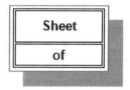

Figure 12 - Sheet Numbering

Enter "1" to the left of the word "of" on both the front and back sides of the first copy of the form. (Note: The back side of each form is clearly marked as such; therefore, both sides of the same form are considered to be the same "Sheet" number.) Sequentially number subsequent copies of the form. When the Square is closed, or at the end of the Season, enter the final Sheet number to the right of the word "of" on all copies of the form. Note, however, that the Weekly Supervisor Log is valid only for the week to which it pertains, so complete the Sheet number block for this form each week.

Note that the sheet number block appears on both the front and back of the Locus Log, Pottery Reading Summary, and Weekly Supervisor Log forms. Since the fronts and backs of all forms are scanned to separate PDF files after the Season ends, it is important that the Sheet number on both sides of these three forms contain the same Sheet number. Otherwise, it would not be possible to tell the back of one form from another.

11.2 Locus Log [LL]

The Locus Log form is used to maintain a sequential, enumerated listing of the Loci that are identified and excavated within the Square. The first Locus in a newly opened Square is, by definition, No. 1. Thereafter, they are numbered sequentially. The Locus Log should be maintained simultaneously with the corresponding Locus forms. The Locus Log is closed when the Square is closed or at the end of the Season, whichever comes first. If the Square is reopened in a subsequent Season, a new Locus Log is started. In this case, the number of the first Locus listed should be the next in sequence from the previously completed Locus Log.

The **Locus Information** data block of the Locus Log form is shown in Figure 13.

LOCUS INFORMATION:						
Locus #	Date Locus Opened (ddmmmyy)	Date Locus Closed (ddmmmyy)	Bucket #s	Locus Description		Estimated Ceramic Stratum*
				Type	Description	

Figure 13 - [LL] Locus Information

Enter the **Locus #** and **Date Locus Opened** <u>before</u> you begin excavating the Locus. At the same time, select and initiate the appropriate Locus Form for this new Locus and enter the form code (shown in brackets in the top right hand corner of the form) without the brackets into **Type**. Also enter a brief **Description** of the Locus.

Examples of **Type** *and* **Description**:

[SL]	"Brown, loose silt/loam w/o artifacts"
[AL]	"Mudbrick wall"
[AL]	"Stone wall forming north side of building"
[AL]	"Builder's trench for stone wall"
[IL]	"Fire pit outlined with stones"
[FSL]	"Stone floor"
[S/BL]	"Dolmen"

The **Estimated Ceramic Stratum** is entered by Senior Staff after the data pertaining to the Square has been analyzed.

The **Locus Information** data block is continued on the back of this form. Use additional copies of this form as needed, being careful to maintain the sequential enumeration of the Locus and Sheet numbers.

11.3 Bench Mark Information [BM]

The Bench Mark Information form is used to record the level and location (relative to other known area features such as the corners of existing Squares) of Bench Marks used for taking level readings within the Square. "Primary" Bench Marks are set by the site surveyor. Always enter the nearest "Primary" Bench Mark on this form.

If the Bench Mark is further away than one Square from where you are taking level reading, then the accuracy of your readings will suffer due to "sag" in the line used with the string level. Therefore, the Square Supervisor may establish "Secondary" Bench Marks closer to the Square being worked whose level is derived either directly or indirectly from a "Primary" Bench Mark. The locations and levels of all Bench Marks used to measure levels in the Square should be recorded on this form in case the Bench Marks are disturbed during the Season by either "night diggers" or grazing animals.

Referring to Figure 14, enter the **Season** (e.g., "2013") and Square **Supervisor**'s first initial and last name for each Bench Mark.

| Season | Supervisor | Bench Mark | | |
		No.	Location References	Level
		P / S		

Figure 14 - [BMI] Bench Mark Information

Number the Bench Marks sequentially and enter the number (**No.**) for each one. Circle **P** if it is a "primary" Bench Mark or **S** if it is a "secondary" Bench Mark.

> Note: The first Bench Mark listed on this form should be the "Primary" Bench Mark that is nearest to the Square. More than one "Primary" Bench Mark may be listed if both were used to measure levels in the Square. If "Secondary" Bench Marks are used, then they should also be listed in this form with a note stating from which previously-established Bench Mark it was derived.

Enter up to two **Location References** for the Bench Mark. For example, if the Bench Mark is one of the stakes used to outline either the west or south edges of Square 45J, then you can simply state the location of the Bench Mark as being "50 cm S of 45J" or "50 cm W of 45J", respectively. (Remember that the SW corner of the Square names the Square, so if you reference that corner, that's all you need to know!)

If the Bench Mark (be it a randomly placed stake or a mark painted on a boulder) is randomly placed relative to the Square grid layout, then enter two **Location References** using the nearest SW corners of two Squares. For example, if the Benchmark a less than 3 m to the west side of Square 42J, measure the distance from the SW corner of Square 42J to the Bench Mark and record it on the first line as "x.xxx m NW of 42J" (where "x.xxx m" is the distance in meters). Then measure the distance from the NW corner of Square 42J (which is also the SW corner of Square 42I) to the Bench Mark and record it on the second line as "x.xxx m SW of 42I". You have now defined the location of the Bench Mark as the intersection of these two measurements.

If the Bench Mark is inside a known Square (assume Square 42J again) and within 3 m of its west side, use the SW and NW corners of that Square as **Location References** and write the two measurements as follows: "x.xxx m NE of 42J" and "x.xxx m SE of 42I".

You should be able to get the **Level** of any Bench Marks set by the Site Surveyor from him. You may establish "Secondary" Bench Marks as needed by carefully measuring their Levels relative to a "Primary" Bench Mark.

11.4 Pottery Reading Summary [PR]

The Pottery Reading Summary form is used to maintain a sequential, enumerated listing of the pottery buckets that are used within a Square. The first pottery bucket in a newly opened Square is, by definition, No. 1. Thereafter, they are numbered sequentially regardless of which Locus they are used in. The Pottery Reading Summary is closed when the Square is closed or at the end of the Season, whichever comes first. If the Square is reopened in a subsequent Season, a new Pottery Reading Summary is started. In this case, the number of the first pottery bucket listed should be the next in sequence from the previously used Pottery Reading Summary.

Pottery buckets should be numbered, tagged (see Section 11.12), and assigned to a Locus <u>before</u> you begin excavating the Locus. A new pottery bucket with a new number and tag should be assigned each day that the Square is actively excavated.

The **Pottery Reading Results** data block of the Pottery Reading Summary form is shown in Figure 15.

Bucket Date (ddmmmyy)	Bucket #	Locus #	# Sherds			Reading Results
			Total	Diag	Kept	

POTTERY READING RESULTS:

Figure 15 - [PR] Pottery Reading Results

Enter the **Bucket Date** (current date; the date on which the pottery bucket is assigned to the Locus). Remember that bucket numbers are assigned sequentially within the context of a Square regardless of what Locus they are used in. Enter the **Bucket #** and **Locus #** to which the bucket is assigned.

The **Total** and **Diag**[nostic] number of sherds (**# Sherds**) contained in the bucket is usually determined at the end of the day by the Square Supervisor. Separate the diagnostic sherds from the others, count them, and enter the number of diagnostic sherds in **Diag**. Also enter this number on the bucket's Pottery Tag (see Section 4.11). Count the non-diagnostic sherds, enter that number on the bucket's Pottery Tag, and enter the total number of sherds (diagnostic plus non-diagnostic) in **Total** on this form.

Bring this form to Pottery Reading each working day. As the dried sherds are "read" (usually the next working day after they were set out to dry), enter the total number of diagnostic pottery sherds that were kept for registration in **Kept**. Pay close attention to the chit-chat around the Pottery Reading table and record in **Reading Results** any comments made about the chronology of the sherds (e.g., "EB1", "MB2", "IA1"). Also write in parentheses the number of diagnostic sherds kept by each chronological period. Sometimes, especially when no diagnostic sherds are kept for registration, the comments may only describe the general trend of the sherds, such as "MB2-ish." Make sure that you write this down, too.

Note: The previous two paragraphs describe the processes that were used during the first eight seasons of the Tall el-Hammam Excavation Project. During Season Nine (2014), pottery processing was delegated to a special team, and pottery readings were more weekly than daily. A new form was created to capture the pottery reading results for later transfer to the Pottery Reading Summary. See Section 11.13 for a description of the new Pottery Reading Record and its intended use in conjunction with the Pottery Reading Summary.

11.5 Weekly Supervisor Log [WS]

The Weekly Supervisor Log form is used to record a weekly journal of the activities that occurred during each week that excavation is conducted in a Square. A new Weekly Supervisor Log should be completed at the end of each week, but it is better to use this form throughout the week as a real-time journal to record significant actions as they happen.

Enter the names of the **Crew Members** in the data block of the Weekly Supervisor Log form shown in Figure 16.

Crew Members	

Figure 16 - [WS] Crew Members

Referring to Figure 17, below, enter the **Date** on which the action occurred along with the **Locus #** in which it occurred. Enter a brief description of the **Action Taken**.

Date (ddmmmyy)	Locus #	Action Taken

Figure 17 - [WS] Actions Taken

Examples of **Action Taken**:

> "Opened locus."
> "Closed locus"
> "Continued excavating locus."
> "Completed excavation; took final photographs and did drawings; closed locus."
> "Found a storage jar broken in place."
> "Found a piriform juglet in tact."

On the back of this form is a 6 x 6 grid in which you should draw a **Rough Sketch** of the square as you left it at the end of the week. This sketch, however, is not a substitute for the official Top Plan drawing that you must do later, but it will help you to remember how things appeared. Use the **Comments** area on the back of this form to record notes to help others interpret your **Rough Sketch** or understand your journal entries under **Action Taken** on the front of the form.

11.6 Soil Locus Form [SL]

The Soil Locus Form is used to record the data pertaining to a Soil Locus. A separate form should be used for each Soil Locus. This form should be initiated before excavation of the Soil Locus begins. **Date Closed** in the **Locus Identification** header should be used to record the date on which excavation of the Locus is completed (i.e., it is completely removed or excavation of the Locus is suspended for the Season), the Square itself is closed (or excavation of the Square is suspended for the Season), or the end of the Season. If the Square and Locus is reopened in a subsequent Season, a new Soil Locus Form should be used with a new Locus number to record the current Season's excavation activity.

Referring to Figure 18, below, enter the **Type of Soil Locus** by blackening the box corresponding to the Locus type. The options are:

☐ **Surface Soil Locus**—the top 5 cm removed from a newly opened Square.

☐ **Cleanup Soil Locus**—the soil removed from a Square that is reopened in the current Season after being initially excavated during a previous Season.

☐ **Analytical Soil Locus**—every other Soil Locus (neither Surface nor Cleanup).

TYPE OF SOIL LOCUS:			
Type of Soil Locus (■ 1):	☐ Surface Soil Locus	☐ Cleanup Soil Locus	☐ Analytical Soil Locus

Figure 18 - [SL] Type of Soil Locus

The **Reason for New Analytical Soil Locus** data block on the Soil Locus Form, shown in Figure 19, applies only to **Analytical Soil Loci**.

REASON FOR NEW ANALYTICAL SOIL LOCUS:					
1. Change in Soil (■ all that apply):	☐ Color	☐ Texture	☐ Consistency	☐ Contents	☐ Not Applicable
2. Diff from Previous Locus Is (■ 1):	☐ Very Clear	☐ Clear	☐ Somewhat Clear	☐ Arbitrary	☐ Not Applicable

Figure 19 - [SL] Reason for New Analytical Soil Locus

The primary reason for defining a new Soil Locus is to account for a change in the soil. The **Change in Soil** options are **Color**, **Texture**, **Consistency**, **Contents**, and **Not Applicable** (explained below). Blacken as many boxes as apply. If **Not Applicable** is blackened, then none of the other four options should be blackened. One reason to select **Not Applicable** is the transition from a Surface Soil Locus to an Analytical Locus, which is done arbitrarily after 5 cm of surface soil has been removed. If you select this option, explain the change in the **Notes** section at the bottom of this form (front side).

Also specify the degree of **Diff**erence **from Previous Locus** by blackening the one box that most closely describes the difference. One reason to select **Not Applicable** is the transition from a Surface Soil Locus to an Analytical Locus, which is done arbitrarily after 5 cm of surface soil has been removed. If you select this option, explain the change in the **Notes** section at the bottom of this form (front side).

The change in the soil is documented in the **Soil Composition** data block of the Soil Locus Form, shown in Figure 20. It is common for the soil in a Locus to be non-uniform. Therefore, up to three **Soil Levels** may be specified to define the **Soil Composition**. The **Soil Levels** are defined as **P**rimary (dominant), **S**econdary (next dominant) and **T**ertiary (least dominant).

Blacken the one box that defines which **Soil Level** you are describing. Since these distinctions may not emerge until excavation of the Locus is underway, the three **Soil Levels** may be entered in any order in this data block, hence the reason for the three options appearing on all three levels.

Soil Color is derived from the *Munsell Soil Color Book*. A sample page from the *Munsell Soil Color Book* is shown in Figure 21. The **Color Code** to be entered into the **Soil Composition** data block consists of the *Munsell Soil Color Book* page number, row number and column number, e.g., 10YR 5/3. The **Color Name** for this **Color Code** is located on the preceding page and, for 10YR 5/3, is "brown."

SOIL COMPOSTION:					
Soil Level* (■ 1)	Soil Color (Use Munsell Soil Color Charts)		Soil Texture (■ one)	Soil Consistency (■ one)	Soil Contents (■ all that apply) (Explain All "Others" in Notes)
	Color Code	Color Name			
□P □S □T			□Silty/Loamy □Clayey □Sandy □Ashy	□Loose □Crushable □Hard	ARTIFACTS: □Pottery □Bone □Shell □Glass □Metal □Lithic □Organic □Other ARCHITECTURAL DEBRIS (fallen or out of place): □Mudbrick □Wall-Stone □Other
□P □S □T			□Silty/Loamy □Clayey □Sandy □Ashy	□Loose □Crushable □Hard	NON-ARCHITECTURAL ROCKS: □Pebbles □Cobbles □Stones □Boulders BURNED MATERIAL: □Ash □Charcoal □Other
□P □S □T			□Silty/Loamy □Clayey □Sandy □Ashy	□Loose □Crushable □Hard	MODERN MATERIAL: □No □Yes_____ OTHER: _____
*P = primary (dominant) soil, S = secondary (next dominant) soil, T = tertiary (least dominant) soil. Mudbrick is not a soil.					

Figure 20 - [SL] Soil Composition

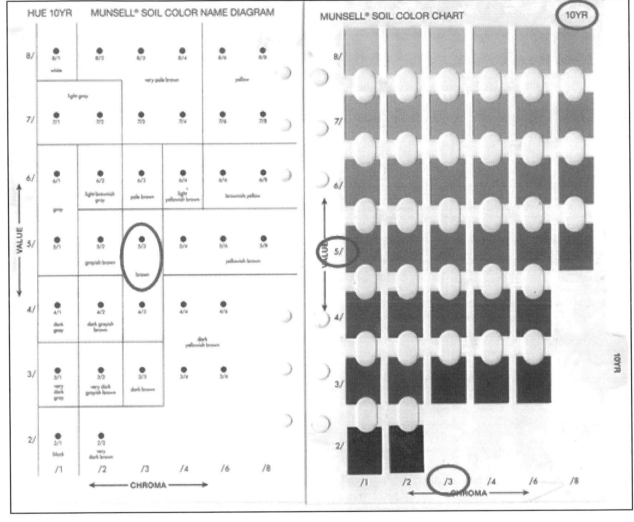

Figure 21 - *Munsell Soil Color Book*

Soil Texture pertains to the "feel" of the soil. Geologically, there are three basic types of soil: clay, silt, and sand. Loam is what we commonly call "dirt." It is so prominent that it is often treated as a basic soil type. There are four options for **Soil Texture** in the **Soil Composition** data block. Blacken the one box that best describes the **Soil Texture**. The four **Soil Texture** options are:

- ☐ **Silty/Loamy**—This is common "dirt" and may contain organic material (decomposed plants, etc). Moist silty/loamy sand will form and retain clumps if squeezed in your closed fist.

- ☐ **Clayey**—Clay, if moist, will form "ribbons" when rolled between the palms of your hands. The better the ribbon that is formed, the higher the clay content of the soil.

- ☐ **Sandy**—Sand is finely crushed rock. It will not form clumps when squeezed in your closed fist.

50

☐ **Ashy**—Ashy soil will be grayish-to-black in color depending upon the organic material that was burned to form the ash.

Soil Consistency in the **Soil Composition** data block pertains to the soil's coherency (whether it sticks together) and hardness of soil particles. In layman's terms:

☐ the soil is **Loose** and does not stick together to form aggregates (clods);

☐ the soil does form aggregates, but is **Crushable** with a bare hand; or

☐ the aggregates are too **Hard** to be crushed by hand.

Blacken the one box that best describes the **Soil Consistency**.

Soil Contents in the **Soil Composition** data block pertains to the non-dirt material found embedded in the soil locus. Blacken as many options as apply. Explain **Other** in the **Notes** section at the bottom of the sheet (front side). **Soil Contents** include:

- **Artifacts** are ancient man-made items consisting of **Pottery**, **Bone**, **Shell**, **Glass**, **Metal**, **Lithic** (stone), **Organic** (e.g., wood) or **Other** materials.

- **Architectural Debris** are materials such as **Mudbrick**, **Wall Stones** (cut and uncut), or **Other** (e.g., timber) used to build structures which have fallen from their original positions.

- Non-Architectural Rocks include:

  ☐ **Pebbles** (up to 7.5 cm) – many fit in one hand

  ☐ **Cobbles** (7.6–24.9 cm) – can carry in one hand

  ☐ **Stones** (25.0–59.9 cm) – takes two hands to carry (a "one-man rock")

  ☐ **Boulders** (60 or more cm) – takes more than one person to move or carry.

- **Burned Material** includes **Ash**, **Charcoal**, and **Other** organic materials that have been exposed to fire.

- **Modern Material** includes trash, plastic, cigarette butts, and anything that you could purchase in a store today.

- **Other**—anything not listed above.

The **Locus Levels**, **Location** and **Relationships** data block, shown in Figure 22, is used to record the level and thickness of the Locus and its spatial orientation to other Loci in the Square.

Use the **Locus Levels** section of this data block to record the **Opening (Top)** and **Closing (Bottom)** levels of the Locus in up to six (6) locations within the Square. This section also provides space to record the information pertaining to the **Bench Mark** that was used as reference for the **Locus Levels**.

- **Loc**ation **Code** refers to the numbers in the small 6 x 6 grid in the **Locus and Level Locations** section of this data block. Each square in the grid represent a one-square-meter section of the Square. Enter the number corresponding to the grid square where you take the level readings.

- The **Opening (Top)** level is the measurement that you take <u>before</u> you begin excavating the Locus.

- The **Closing (Bottom)** level is the measurement that you take <u>after</u> you finish excavating the Locus.

- **Diff**erence is the arithmetic difference (absolute value) between the **Opening** and **Closing** levels and represents the thickness of the Locus.

LOCUS LEVELS:				LOCUS LOCATION:						LOCUS RELATIONSHIPS:	
Loc. Code*	Opening (Top)	Closing (Bottom)	Diff.	Locus and Level Locations						Relation-ships	Locus or Square/Locus #s**
				1	2	3	4	5	6	Under	
				7	8	9	10	11	12	Over	
				13	14	15	16	17	18	Abuts	
				19	20	21	22	23	24	Equals	
				25	26	27	28	29	30	Cuts	
				31	32	33	34	35	36	Cut By	
Bench Mark:		No:		Level:				Location:			

*Location Code—Use codes 1-36 to show the location of the levels. **Use square/locus #s under "Equals" if the locus is in a different square.

Figure 22 - [SL] Locus Levels, Location, and Relationships

Use the 6 x 6 grid in the **Locus Location** section of this data block to draw a rough sketch of the Locus within the Square. Use a highlighter or colored pencil to distinguish the Locus from the rest of the Square.

Transcribe the **Bench Mark** number (**No**), **Level**, and **Location** from the **Bench Mark Information** Form (see Section 11.3) for the bench mark that was used to measure the **Locus Levels**.

The **Locus Relationships** section of this data block is used to describe the spatial relationship of the Locus to other Loci in this or neighboring Squares. If the related Locus is in this Square, just enter the Locus number. If the related Locus is in another Square, then enter both the Square and related Locus numbers (e.g., "LS45K/3"). The spatial **Relationships** are:

- ☐ **Under**—This Soil Locus is under what other Locus/Loci, if any, in the Square?

- ☐ **Over**—This Soil Locus is over what other Locus/Loci, if any, in the Square?

- ☐ **Abuts**—This Soil Locus is at the same level and abuts what other Locus/Loci, if any, in the Square?

- ☐ **Equals**—This Soil Locus is equivalent to what other Soil Locus/Loci, if any, in this Square or an adjacent Square?

☐ **Cuts**—This Soil Locus cuts through by what other Locus/Loci, if any, in the Square?

☐ **Cut By**—This Soil Locus is cut through by what other Locus/Loci, if any, in the Square?

The **Bucket Contents** data block, shown in Figure 23, is on the back side of the Soil Locus Form.

Date (ddmmmyy)	Bucket #	General #s		Specific Objects (Significant Artifacts)		
		# Sherds	# Bones	Object Description	# Items	Level (at lowest point)

Figure 23 - [SL] Bucket Contents

The **Date** and **Bucket #** should be transcribed to this form from the **Pottery Reading Summary** form at the same time that the **Pottery Tag** is initiated and attached to the Pottery Bucket.

The [Total] **# Sherds** should be transcribed to this form from the **Pottery Reading Summary** form after it is entered there (see Section 11.4).

The **# Bones** is usually small enough to count in the field. If so, then enter this count before leaving the site for the day; otherwise, since bones are not washed, count the bones and enter the number when you get back to the washing station after setting the sherds to soak.

Specific Objects (Significant Artifacts) such as small complete pottery vessels should be placed in a mesh bag and affixed with an **Identification Tag** (see Section 11.11). Also, if you find a pottery vessel broken in place and the collection of sherds is small enough to fit in a mesh bag, tag the bag with an **Identification Tag**. If the collection of sherds from a single vessel will not fit in a mesh bag, then place the sherds in a separate Pottery Bucket and affix the **Identification Tag** to the handle. Write a brief **Object Description** and the **# Items** in the mesh bag or separate Pottery Bucket if there are too many sherds to fit in a mesh bag. Measure the **Level** at the lowest point from where the object was removed and enter that number into the form.

> *Note: Since most objects are fragile, do not place them in the Pottery Bucket after bagging and tagging. Instead, keep them on or under the Square Supervisor's Field Table until the end of the day. Place the mesh bags in the top of the corresponding Pottery Buckets before leaving the site for the day.*

The **Photographs** data block is shown in Figure 24. Every Locus and feature should be photographed, and every object (i.e., significant artifact) should be photographed *in situ* before it is removed from the Locus. Use this data block for recording official photographs taken by the Excavation Photographer only. (You may take as many pictures as you want with your own camera, but use your personal journal to record them.)

PHOTOGRAPHS:			
Date (ddmmmyy)	Photo #	Direction*	Subject

Figure 24 - [SL] Photographs

Enter the **Date** on which the photograph was taken. The Excavation Photographer will tell you the **Photo #**. (If he doesn't, be sure to ask him for it!)

Use "Eight-Point Compass" notation (N, NE, E, SE, S, SW, W, NW) to enter the **Direction** that the Excavation Photographer was facing when he snapped the picture.

Enter a brief description of the **Subject** of the photograph.

The **Samples** data block, shown in Figure 25, is used to account for any samples taken for special handling. In each box, enter the date (e.g., 15JAN13) that each sample was taken. In addition to entering the date on which the sample was taken, also write a brief description of the sample in the **Notes** section at the bottom of the front side of this form.

SAMPLES (Show date(s) each sample was collected in ddmmmyy format)				
Dry Soil	Water-Screening	Flotation	Radiocarbon	Other_____

Figure 25 - [SL] Samples

The purposes for which **Samples** that might be taken include:

- **Dry Soil**—a soil sample taken for microscopic analysis.

- **Water-Screening**—a soil sample whose components will be separated using water and fine screens.

- **Flotation**—a soil sample containing organic materials that will be separated (floated) from the non-organic material with water.

- **Radiocarbon**—a piece or organic material (e.g., charcoal) at least 2 cubic cm in volume that will be carbon-dated.

- **Other**—any purpose not listed above such as a soil sample taken for chemical analysis.

The **Stratigraphic Analysis** data block, shown in Figure 26, contains information on the cultural stratum in which the Locus is placed. *This data block is completed by senior staff only* after all data on this Locus (e.g., pottery, artifacts, and features) and all Loci within a cultural stratum have been analyzed.

STRATIGRAPHIC ANALYSIS (Completed by senior staff only)			
Stratum			**Interpretation/Comments**
Period	**Sub-Period**	**Phase**	

Figure 26 - [SL] Stratigraphic Analysis

11.7 Architectural Locus Form [AL]

The Architectural Locus Form is used to record the data pertaining to an Architectural Locus. A separate form should be used for each Architectural Locus. This form should be initiated before excavation of the Architectural Locus begins. The "Date Closed" should be used to record the date on which excavation of the Locus is completed (i.e., it is completely removed or excavation of the Locus is suspended for the Season), the Square itself is closed (or excavation of the Square is suspended for the Season), or the end of the Season. If the Square and Locus is reopened in a subsequent Season, a new Architectural Locus Form should be used (with a new Locus number) to record the current Season's excavation activity.

> *Note: Walls that are clearly abutting upon discovery should be treated as separate Loci. Also, straight-line wall segments that meet at a 90-degree (more or less) angle should be treated as separate Loci.*

Several of the data blocks on this form are identical to what are also contained on the Soil Locus Form. Where this is the case, only the differences (if any) will be noted.

The **Wall Construction** data block, shown in Figure 27, is used to record the materials and construction method used to construct the wall.

WALL CONSTRUCTION:

Material	Construction Style	Dominant Size	Mortar	Wall Finish ↓Inside Outside↓	Mudbrick Composition
□ Mudbrick	□ Head/Stretch □ Stacked □ Tied □ Other	**(cm)** L:_____ W:_____ T:_____	□ None (Dry) □ Mud/Clay □ Mud/Clay/Ash □ Other	□ Mud/Clay □ □ Plaster □ □ Other □ □ Unknown □	**Main Ingredient:** □ Mud □ Clay □ Huwar □ Other
□ Masonry 　□ Unworked 　　Fieldstones 　□ Worked 　　Fieldstones	□ Chinked □ Rubble-Filled □ Rubble □ Other	**%** ____Cobbles (7.6-24.9 cm) ____Stones (25.0-59.9 cm) ____Boulders (60.0+ cm)	□ None (Dry) □ Mud/Clay □ Mud/Clay/Ash □ Other	□ None □ □ Mud/Clay □ □ Mud/Clay/Ash □ □ Plaster □ □ Other □	**Temper/Binder:** □ Straw □ Pottery Sherds □ Pebbles □ Other □ Unknown
□ Dressed/ 　Ashlar 　Blocks	□ Head/Stretch □ Orthostat □ Quoin & Pier □ Rubble-Filled □ Other	**(cm)** L:_____ W:_____ T:_____	□ None (Dry) □ Mud/Clay □ Cement □ Other	□ None □ □ Plaster □ □ Other □	**Munsell Color Code:** _____ **Munsell Description:** _____

Figure 27 - |AL| Wall Construction

At Tall el-Hammam, there are only two basic classifications of **Material** used in Architectural Loci, as defined below:

□ **Mudbrick**—Mudbricks basically are made of soil, such as, mud, clay, or huwar (a soft, chalky limestone) and some sort of temper or binder for strength, such as straw, pottery sherds, or pebbles.

□ **Masonry**—Three different types of **Masonry** are found at Tall el-Hammam:

□ **Unworked Fieldstones**—Natural stones unworked by humans.

□ **Worked** Fieldstones—Natural stones that are worked somewhat by humans to fit securely with a minimum amount of chinkstones.

□ **Dressed/Ashlar** Blocks—Stones that are clearly shaped into rectangular blocks with square corners and edges between surfaces and an excellent fit so that chinkstones are not needed.

Blacken the box that best describes the **Material** used in the construction.

Mudbricks are called "stretchers" or "headers" according to how they are laid relative to the line of the wall. Referring to Figure 28, if laid lengthwise along the line of the wall, they are called "stretchers"; if laid crosswise to the line of the wall, they are called "headers".

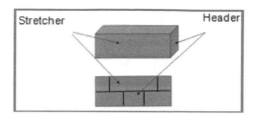

Figure 28 - Mudbrick Orientation

Mudbrick Construction Styles are defined according to how the mudbricks are laid. The variations in **Mudbrick Construction Styles** are:

☐ **Head/Stretch**—There are two methods of laying mudbricks as overlapping headers and stretcher, as shown in Figures 29 and 30:

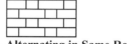

Figure 29 - Alternating in Same Row

Figure 30 - Alternating Rows

☐ **Stacked**—No attempt is made to overlap the mudbricks, as shown in Figure 31.

Figure 31 - Stacked

☐ **Tied**—Overlapping; laid as all stretchers (shown in Figure 32) or all headers.

Figure 32 - Overlapping

☐ **Other**—None of the above; explain in the **Notes** section at the top of the back side of this form.

Blacken the one box that best describes the **Mudbrick Construction Style** used in the construction.

Masonry Construction Styles using Fieldstones include:

☐ **Chinked (or Boulder and Chink)**—The wall is composed largely of worked or unworked cobbles, stones, or boulders with smaller chinkstones wedged between giving stability to the wall, as shown in Figure 33.

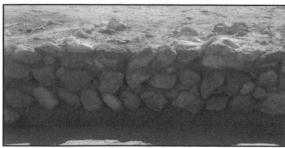

Figure 33 - Chinked Wall Construction

57

- ☐ **Rubble-Filled**—The space between two outer rows of stones and/or boulders (may or may not be chinked) filled with rubble (a mixture of dirt, pebbles and cobbles).

- ☐ **Rubble**—The wall is constructed solely of rubble without any attempt to form courses (layers).

- ☐ **Other**—None of the above; explain in the **Notes** section at the top of the back side of this form.

Blacken as many boxes as needed to describe the **Masonry Construction Style** using **Fieldstones**.

Masonry Construction Styles using Dressed/Ashlar Blocks include:

- ☐ **Head/Stretch**— **Dressed/Ashlar Blocks** may be laid using the same methods as for laying mudbricks (see above).

- ☐ **Orthostat**—a large, thin ashlar block set on its edge or end, such as the ashlar blocks on either side of the doorway in Figure 34.

Source: http://www.thefreedictionary.com
Figure 34 - Orthostat

- ☐ **Quoin & Pier**—pronounced "coin and peer"—A method of construction in which uncut fieldstones (quoins) are wedged between vertical ashlar pillars (piers). The piers are often at intervals of two-to-four meters with the intervening spaces filled with fieldstones, as shown in Figure 35.

Source: Excavation Manual: Madaba Plains Project
Figure 35 - Quoin & Pier

- ☐ **Rubble-Filled**—Similar to quoin and pier walls, except that the space between two parallel, outer rows of ashlar blocks is filled with rubble.

- ☐ **Other**—None of the above; explain in the **Notes** section at the top of the back side of this form.

Blacken the one box that best describes the **Masonry Construction Style** using **Dressed/Ashlar Blocks**.

For **Mudbrick** and **Dressed/Ashlar Blocks**, enter the **Dominant Size** (most common size) of the length (**L**), width (**W**) and thickness (**T**) measured in centimeters. For **Fieldstones**, estimate the relative percentages of **Cobbles**, **Stones**, and **Boulders** in a 1-2 m length of the wall.

Blacken the box that most closely describes the type of **Mortar** used in the **Wall Construction**. The options are:

- ☐ None—The Mudbricks, Fieldstones or Dressed/Ashlar Blocks were "dry-stacked" without using any Mortar.

- ☐ **Mud/Clay**—A combination of mud and clay was used as **Mortar**.

- ☐ **Mud/Clay/Ash**—Similar to mud and clay, except that the ash content gives the **Mortar** a grayish-to-black color. (Not found in **Dressed/Ashlar Blocks** wall construction.)

- ☐ **Cement**—A substance that hardens like stone. Ancient cement was often softer than our modern varieties. (Applies only to **Dressed/Ashlar Blocks** wall construction.)

- ☐ **Other**—None of the above; explain in the **Notes** section at the top of the back side of this form.

A **Wall Finish** may be applied to the outside, inside, or both of a wall. Blacken the option that best describes the type of **Wall Finish** used:

- ☐ **None**—The wall does not have a finish on either side. **Fieldstone** walls might not have had a finish. **Dressed/Ashlar Block** walls probably did not have a finish on the outside, but may have plaster on the inside. **Mudbrick** walls always had a finish to protect them, so blackening the **None** box is not applicable (see **Unknown**).

- ☐ **Mud/Clay**—The finish is made of mud and clay.

- ☐ **Mud/Clay/Ash**—The finish is made of mud, clay and ash. The ash gives the finish a grayish-to-black color.

- ☐ **Plaster**—Plaster can be almost as hard as cement. Its basic composition includes lime or chalk and can be combined with varying proportions of mud and sand.

- ☐ **Unknown**—The wall probably had a finish, but the finish is not discernible. All **Mudbrick** walls in ancient times had a finish to protect the **Mudbrick** from the elements, especially moisture. Therefore, if a **Mudbrick** wall is found and the finish is not discernible, blacken the **Unknown** box.

- ☐ **Other**—None of the above; explain in the **Notes** section at the top of the back side of this form.

The **Mudbrick Composition** section of the **Wall Construction** data block applies, obviously, only to walls made with **Mudbrick**. Blacken the one box that best describes the **Main Ingredient** of the **Mudbrick**—**Mud, Clay, Huwar,** or **Other** (explain in the **Notes** section on the back side of the form). Blacken the one box that best describes the

Temper/Binder of the **Mudbrick—Straw**, **Pottery Sherds**, **Pebbles**, **Other** (explain in the **Notes** section on the back side of the form), or **Unknown** (something is there, but you don't know what it is).

Use the *Munsell Soil Color Book* to determine the **Color Code** and **Description** for the **Mudbrick.** (See Figure 21 in Section 11.6 for instructions on how to use the *Munsell Soil Color Book*.)

The **Architectural Locus Relationships** data block is shown in Figure 36. Use this section to define the spatial relationships of this Locus to other Architectural Loci, which include:

ARCHITECTURAL LOCUS RELATIONSHIPS	
Relationship	Locus # or Square/Locus #
Bonding Walls	
Abutting Walls	
Foundation Wall	
Superstructure Wall	
Foundation Trench	
Associated FL/Surf.	
Extends into Abutting Square(s) as Locus(i)*	

Figure 36 - [AL] Architectural Locus Relationships

- **Bonding Walls**—Both this wall and the associated wall (identify by its Locus #) meet at an indistinguishable junction.

- **Abutting Walls**—There is a clear seam between this wall and the associated wall (identify by Locus #).

- **Foundation Wall**—This wall (typically made of stone) lies below and supports another wall (typically made of mudbrick) that forms the superstructure of the building (identify by Locus #).

- **Superstructure Wall**—This wall (typically made of mudbrick) sits on top of another (typically made of stone) wall that serves as a foundation (identify by Locus #).

- **Foundation Trench**—The foundation trench is considered an Installation Locus (see Section 11.9). It is a trench cut into the ground to provide a level surface on which to lay a foundation wall. After the foundation wall is constructed, the foundation trench is typically filled with a soil matrix that appears different in color, texture, or content from the surrounding Soil Loci (see Section 11.6).

- **Associated Floor/Surface**—Floors and other surfaces are considered to be a special case of Architectural Loci. Identify the Locus # of any floor, courtyard surface, pathway or road that abuts this wall, if any.

- **Extends into Abutting Square(s) as Locus**—This wall extends beyond the perimeter of this Square. Identify the abutting Square(s) and corresponding Locus #(s).

Enter the corresponding **Locus #** if in the same Square, or **Square/Locus #** if in an abutting Square.

The **Non-Architectural Locus Relationships** data block, shown in Figure 37, is use to define the spatial relationships of this Architectural Locus to non-Architectural Loci, which include Soil Loci, Installation Loci and Skeleton/Burial Loci. (Note: Functional Surface Loci are considered to be a special case of Architectural Loci as noted above.) This data block is identical to the **Locus Relationships** data block on the Soil Locus Form (see Figure 22 in Section 11.6).

NON-ARCHITECTURAL LOCUS RELATIONSHIPS	
Relationship	Locus Numbers
Under	
Over	
Abuts	
Cuts	
Cut By	

Figure 37 - [AL] Non-Architectural Locus Relationships

The **Locus Levels** and **Locus Location** data block, shown in Figure 38, is identical the corresponding data block on the Soil Locus Form (see Figure 22 in Section 11.6). If you are instructed to leave the wall in place, then postpone taking the **Closing** levels until after you locate the bottom of the wall by excavating the abutting Soil or Functional Surface Loci to the bottom of the wall.

LOCUS LEVELS:				LOCUS LOCATION:					
Loc. Code*	Opening (Top)	Closing (Bottom)	Diff.	Locus and Level Locations					
				1	2	3	4	5	6
				7	8	9	10	11	12
				13	14	15	16	17	18
				19	20	21	22	23	24
				25	26	27	28	29	30
				31	32	33	34	35	36

Figure 38 - [AL] Locus Levels and Locations

The **Overall Wall Size** data block, shown in Figure 39, is used to record the wall dimensions within the Square. Dimensions to be measured include:

- **Length**—For walls that extend beyond the Square in both directions, measure the length of the wall from the center point of the wall at the Square boundaries. For walls that turn a sharp corner within the Square, each wall segment should be treated as a separate Locus. (You may choose which segment includes the outside corner, with the other segment "bonded" to it.) Measure the center-line length of each wall segment.

OVERALL WALL SIZE:	
Dimension	Size
Length (m) (within square)	
Thickness (cm)	Max: Min:
Height (cm)	Max: Min:
# of Existing Courses (i.e., # rows high)	Max: Min: □ Cannot Be Determined

Figure 39 - [AL] Overall Wall Size

- **Thickness**—Measure and record the **Max**imum and **Min**imum thickness of the wall.

- **Height**—Enter the **Max**imum and **Min**imum **Locus Level** differences.

- **# of Existing Courses**—Enter the **Max**imum and **Min**imum number of courses (rows/layers) of wall material. If you are instructed to leave the wall in place, then postpone entering this data until after you locate the bottom of the wall by excavating the abutting Soil or Functional Surface Loci to the bottom of the wall. If you do not reach the bottom of the wall by the time the Square is closed at the end of the Season, only then should you blacken the **Cannot be Determined** box.

The **Bucket Contents** data block on the back side of the Architectural Locus Form is identical to the same block on the Soil Locus Form (see Figure 23 in Section 11.6).

The **Photographs** data block on the back side of the Architectural Locus Form is identical to the same block on the Soil Locus Form (see Figure 24 in Section 11.6).

The **Samples** data block on the back side of the Architectural Locus Form is identical to the same block on the Soil Locus Form (see Figure 25 in Section 11.6).

The **Stratigraphic Analysis** data block on the back side of the Architectural Locus Form is identical to the same block on the Soil Locus Form (see Figure 26 in Section 11.6).

11.8 Functional Surface Locus Form [FSL]

The Functional Surface Locus Form is used to record the data pertaining to a Functional Surface Locus such as a floor, courtyard, path or road. A separate form should be used for each Functional Surface Locus no matter how small it might be within the Square. This form should be initiated before excavation of the Functional Surface Locus begins. The "Date Closed" should be used to record the date on which excavation of the Locus is completed (i.e., it is completely removed, or excavation of the Locus is suspended for the Season), the Square itself is closed (or excavation of the Square is suspended for the Season), or the end of the Season. If the Square and Locus is reopened in a subsequent Season, a new Functional Surface Locus Form should be used (with a new Locus number) to record the current Season's excavation activity.

The **Reason for New Functional Surface Focus** data block on this form is identical to the **Reason for New Soil Focus** data block on the Soil Locus Form (see Figure 19 in Section 11.6).

The **Functional Surface Material and Characteristics** data block, shown in Figure 40, is used to record the materials used in making the Functional Surface and their characteristics.

Blacken as many boxes as needed to describe the **Material** used to construct the Functional Surface. These materials will typically include soil materials (**Beaten Earth**, **Lime**, **Plaster** or **Huwar**), masonry materials (**Mudbrick**, **Baked Brick** or **Terrera/Mosaic**), or fieldstones (**Crushed Rock/Pebbles**, **Cobble**, **Stone** or **Boulder**). If any **Other** material is used, explain it in the **Notes** section at the bottom of this form.

FUNCTIONAL SURFACE MATERIAL AND CHARACTERISTICS (■ all that apply):			
Material	Dominant Size	Munsell Color Code	Munsell Description
□ Beaten Earth	XXXXXXXXXXXXXXXXXXXX		
□ Lime	XXXXXXXXXXXXXXXXXXXX		
□ Plaster	XXXXXXXXXXXXXXXXXXXX		
□ Huwar	XXXXXXXXXXXXXXXXXXXX		
□ Mudbrick	L: W: T: cm		
□ Baked Brick	L: W: T: cm		
□ Tessera (Mosaic)	L: W: T: cm		
□ Crushed Rock/Pebbles	(<=7.5 cm) _____ %	XXXXXXXXXX	XXXXXXXXXXXXXXXXXXX
□ Cobble	(7.6-24.9 cm) _____ %	XXXXXXXXXX	XXXXXXXXXXXXXXXXXXX
□ Stone	(25.0-59.9 cm) _____ %	XXXXXXXXXX	XXXXXXXXXXXXXXXXXXX
□ Boulder	(60.0+ cm) _____ %	XXXXXXXXXX	XXXXXXXXXXXXXXXXXXX
□ Other:			

Figure 40 - [FSL] Functional Surface Material and Characteristics

Dominant Size is irrelevant for soil materials, so these cells of the data block grid are X'd out. For masonry materials, enter the average **L**ength, **W**idth and **T**hickness in centimeters.

For fieldstones, estimate the relative percentages of each size listed within a 1-square-meter area.

Use the *Munsell Soil Color Book* to determine the **Color Code** and **Description** for the soil and masonry materials. (See Figure 21 in Section 11.6 for instructions on how to use the *Munsell Soil Color Book*.) Note that color does not apply to fieldstones, so these cells of the data block grid are X'd out.

The **Locus Levels**, **Locus Location** and **Locus Relationships** data block on this form is identical the corresponding data block on the Soil Locus Form (see Figure 22 in Section 11.6).

The **Bucket Contents** data block on the back side of the Architectural Locus Form is identical to the same block on the Soil Locus Form (see Figure 23 in Section 11.6).

The **Photographs** data block on the back side of this form is identical to the same block on the Soil Locus Form (see Figure 24 in Section 11.6).

The **Samples** data block on the back side of this form is identical to the same block on the Soil Locus Form (see Figure 25 in Section 11.6).

The **Stratigraphic Analysis** data block on the back side of this form is identical to the same block on the Soil Locus Form (see Figure 26 in Section 11.6).

11.9 Installation Locus Form [IL]

The Installation Locus Form is used to record the data pertaining to an Installation Locus. A separate form should be used for each Installation Locus. This form should be initiated before excavation of the Installation Locus begins. The "Date Closed" should be used to record the date on which excavation of the Locus is completed (i.e., it is completely removed or excavation of the Locus is suspended for the Season), the Square itself is closed (or excavation of the Square is suspended for the Season), or the end of the Season. If the Square and Locus is reopened in a subsequent Season, a new Installation Locus Form should be used (with a new Locus number) to record the current Season's excavation activity.

The **Type of Installation** data block, shown in Figure 41, is used to define the type of installation.

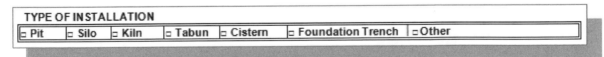

TYPE OF INSTALLATION

□ Pit   □ Silo   □ Kiln   □ Tabun   □ Cistern   □ Foundation Trench   □ Other

Figure 41 - [IL] Type of Installation

Blacken the one box that most closely represents type of installation. The six options are: **Pit** (dug into the ground; includes a stone-lined fire/cooking pit), **Silo** (installed above ground), **Kiln** (for firing pottery), **Tabun** (for cooking food), **Cistern** (for storing water), **Foundation Trench** (used to provide a level surface for a foundation wall), or **Other**. If

Other is blackened, write in a brief description or explain in the **Notes** section at the bottom of the form.

The **Installation Characteristics** data block, shown in Figure 41, is used to define the **Material** used to construct the Installation, its **Shape**, and its **Measurements**.

INSTALLATION CHARACTERISTICS (■ all that apply):		
MATERIAL	SHAPE	MEASUREMENTS
□ Beaten Earth	□ Linear	
□ Lime	□ Curvilinear	Length (greatest)
□ Plaster	□ Rectangular	Width (greatest)
□ Huwar	□ Triangular	or Thickness (average)
□ Mudbrick	□ Circular	Height
□ Baked Brick	□ Semi-Circular	Orientation of long axis:
□ Tessera	□ Oval	□ N □ NE □ E □ SE
□ Crushed Pebbles	□ Irregular	□ S □ SW □ W □ NW
□ Cobble	□ Other:	□ n/a (circular only)
□ Stone		
□ Boulder		
□ Other:		

Figure 42 - [IL] Installation Characteristics

Blacken as many boxes as needed to describe the **Material** used to construct the Installation. These materials will typically include soil materials (**Beaten Earth**, **Lime**, **Plaster** or **Huwar**), masonry materials (**Mudbrick**, **Baked Brick** or **Terrera/Mosaic**), or fieldstones (**Crushed Rock/Pebbles**, **Cobble**, **Stone** or **Boulder**). If any **Other** material is used, explain it in the **Notes** section at the bottom of this form.

Blacken the one box that best describes the **Shape** of the Installation. The options are:

☐ **Linear**—a reasonably straight line

☐ **Curvilinear**—sort of straight, but with some curves

☐ **Rectangular**—four-sided; includes square

☐ **Triangular**—three-sided

☐ **Circular**—a closed circle (may include a small opening for internal access)

☐ **Semi-Circular**—a partial circle (at least half)

☐ **Oval**—a closed oval (may include a small opening for internal access)

☐ **Irregular**—no discernible shape as described above

☐ **Other**—none of the above; explain in the **Notes** section at the bottom of this form.

Refer to Figure 43 for examples of how to take **Length** and **Width Measurements**. Measure the longest straight-line, end-to-end distances for the **Length** of "open" Installations (see Curvilinear in Figure 43). The **Length** will always be greater of the **Width** regardless of the orientation of the Installation. If the Installation has definite walls to it, then also measure and record the average **Thickness**.

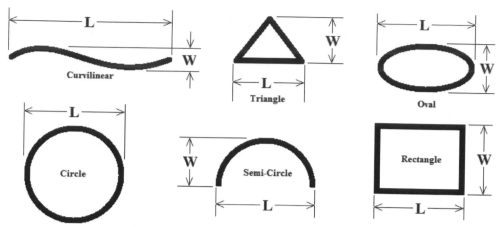

Figure 43 - [IL] Installation Measurements

The **Locus Levels**, **Locus Location** and **Locus Relationships** data block on this form is identical the corresponding data block on the Soil Locus Form (see Figure 22 in Section 11.6).

The **Bucket Contents** data block on the back side of the Architectural Locus Form is identical to the same block on the Soil Locus Form (see Figure 23 in Section 11.6).

The **Photographs** data block on the back side of this form is identical to the same block on the Soil Locus Form (see Figure 24 in Section 11.6).

The **Samples** data block on the back side of this form is identical to the same block on the Soil Locus Form (see Figure 25 in Section 11.6).

The **Stratigraphic Analysis** data block on the back side of this form is identical to the same block on the Soil Locus Form (see Figure 26 in Section 11.6).

11.10 Skeleton/Burial Locus Form [S/BL]

The Skeleton/Burial Locus Form is used to record the data pertaining to a Skeleton/Burial Locus. A separate form should be used for each Skeleton/Burial Locus. This form should be initiated before excavation of the Skeleton/Burial Locus begins. The "Date Closed" should be used to record the date on which excavation of the Locus is completed (i.e., it is completely removed or excavation of the Locus is suspended for the Season), the Square itself is closed (or excavation of the Square is suspended for the Season), or the end of the Season. If the Square and Locus is reopened in a subsequent Season, a new Skeleton/Burial Locus Form should be used (with a new Locus number) to record the current Season's excavation activity.

A **Burial** (also called an "inhumation") Locus is the purposeful placement of the body or the skeletal remains of a body in a grave, tomb or container. A **Skeleton (Non-Burial)** Locus is a skeleton found where the body fell at death as a result of injury (like a wall falling on the person during an earthquake) or battle. Blacken the box that describes the type of inhumation, as shown in Figure 44.

□ BURIAL	□ SKELETON (NON-BURIAL)

Figure 44 - [S/BL] Type of Inhumation

If the inhumation is a **Burial**, then blacken the one box that best describes the **Container** in which the skeleton was found (see Figure 45). The **Container** options are:

□ **Unlined Pit**—The body was placed in a hole dug into the ground for burial.

□ **Stone-Lined Pit**—The hole in the ground was lined with stones before the body was placed in it.

□ **Tomb**—The body was placed in a natural or man-made cave or a constructed tomb or mausoleum.

□ **Ossuary**—The bones of the deceased were collected and placed in a box-shaped container made of stone or pottery.

□ **Jar**—The bones of the deceased were collected and placed in a jar-shaped container made of stone or pottery.

□ **Sarcophagus**—The body was placed in a body-sized container.

□ **Other**—Provide a short description; continue in the **Notes** section on the back of this form if necessary.

CONTAINER (if Burial):					
□ Unlined Pit	□ Stone-lined Pit	□ Tomb	□ Ossuary	□ Jar	□ Sarcophagus
□ Other:					

Figure 45 - [S/BL] Burial Container

The **Special Characteristics** data block, shown in Figure 46, is used to record aspects that characterize the inhumation of the body or skeleton.

SPECIAL CHARACTERISTICS (■ all that apply):		
ACCESSIBILITY	DISPOSAL	ARTICULATION
□ Totally in Square	□ Primary Inhumation	□ Completely Articulated
□ Head in _____ Balk	□ Secondary Inhumation	□ Articulated
□ Upper Half in _____ Balk	□ Cremation	□ Semi-Articulated
□ Lower Half in _____ Balk	□ Multiple Burials	□ Disarticulated
□ Lower Legs in _____ Balk	Total Burials:	□ Completely Disarticulated
□ Other:	□ Other:	□ Fragments Only

Figure 46 - [S/BL] Special Characteristics

The **Accessibility** section of the **Special Characteristics** data block is used to describe the placement of the skeletal remains within the boundaries of the Square. If the skeleton is totally in the Square, then blacken that box. If the skeleton is only partially within the Square, then blacken the corresponding box to note which balk (**N/S/E/W**) is concealing

67

part of the skeleton. If **Other** is selected (e.g., the bones are scattered over multiple Squares), then explain in the **Notes** section on the back of this form.

The **Disposal** section of the **Special Characteristics** data block is used to record the nature of the burial. Blacken the box that best describes the **Disposal** of the remains. The options are:

☐ **Primary Inhumation**—The skeleton is found in the position and location in which the body was laid to rest.

☐ **Secondary Inhumation**—The skeleton was relocated after the soft tissue was removed by either decay or wild animals or birds. Note that this is the option to select whenever bones are found in an **Ossuary** or **Jar**.

☐ **Cremation**—Select this option when a **Jar** containing ash is found in a burial context.

☐ **Multiple Burials**—Blacken this box if multiple skeletons are found in the same Locus and enter the number of skeletons found.

☐ **Other**—If you blacken this option, explain in the **Notes** section on the back of this form.

The **Articulation** section of the **Special Characteristics** data block is used to record the positioning of the bones. Blacken the box that best describes the **Articulation** of the remains. The options are:

☐ **Completely Articulated**—Virtually all of the bones are found in their natural end-to-end positions.

☐ **Articulated**—Most of the bones are found in their natural end-to-end positions.

☐ **Semi-Articulated**—At least half of the bones are found in their natural end-to-end positions.

☐ **Disarticulated**—Only some (less than half) of the bones are found in their natural end-to-end positions.

☐ **Completely Disarticulated**—Either the bones are scattered over a broad area, or the bones were found in an **Ossuary** or **Jar**.

☐ **Fragments Only**—Either only partial bones are found, or this is a **Cremation** burial.

Special Characteristics are continued in the **Statistics**, **Body Position** and **Orientation** data block shown in Figure 47.

STATISTICS:	BODY POSITION:	ORIENTATION (FACING):	
Est. Age:	☐ Extended	☐ North	☐ South
Sex:	☐ Loosely Flexed	☐ East	☐ West
	☐ Tightly Flexed	☐ Up	☐ Down
	☐ Unknown		

Figure 47 - [S/BL] Statistics, Position and Orientation

Unless you are highly trained in human anatomy or osteopathy, you will have to defer to one of the team specialists to enter the **Est**imated **Age** and **Sex** in the **Statistics** section of this data block.

Blacken the one block that best describes the **Body Position** of the skeleton. The options are:

☐ **Extended**—There is no folding of the legs, as is usually the case when a body is laid to rest flat on its back. (The arms may be or may not be crossed on the chest.)

☐ **Loosely Flexed**—There is a visible bending of the legs at the hips and knees, as is usually the case when a body is laid to rest on its side. This position prevents the body from rolling. The arms will usually be loosely flexed as well, with the hands in front of the sternum.

☐ **Tightly Flexed**—The legs are tightly flexed with the knees up against the rib cage. The arms will typically be tightly folded to the outside of the legs with the hands near the chin. This is sometimes called the "prenatal position."

☐ **Unknown**—Blacken this option if the leg bones are disarticulated or scattered, or the skeleton (or the ashes thereof) is found in an **Ossuary** or **Jar**.

Blacken the one or more blocks to describe the **Orientation** of the skeleton. Base this decision on the orientation of the skull, if present, or the general direction in which the sternum (front of the rib cage) faces. The options are the four cardinal directions (**North/South/East/West**), Face-**Up** or Face-**Down**. Blacken two boxes to indicate the intermediate directions for an 8-point compass (e.g., blacken both **North** and **East** to indicate Northeast). If the skeleton is either Face-**Up** or Face-**Down**, also blacken the compass point direction(s) to indicate the alignment of the spine (based on the neck vertebrae, not the coccyx/tailbone).

The **Locus Levels**, **Locus Location** and **Locus Relationships** data block on this form is identical the corresponding data block on the Soil Locus Form (see Figure 22 in Section 11.6).

The **Bucket Contents** data block on the back side of the Architectural Locus Form is identical to the same block on the Soil Locus Form (see Figure 23 in Section 11.6).

The **Photographs** data block on the back side of this form is identical to the same block on the Soil Locus Form (see Figure 24 in Section 11.6).

The **Stratigraphic Analysis** data block on the back side of this form is identical to the same block on the Soil Locus Form (see Figure 26 in Section 11.6).

11.11 Identification Tag

The Identification Tag, shown in Figure 48, is attached to each object that is excavated from a Locus. If small enough to be placed in a net bag, the tag is attached to the bag. If the "object" is a bucket full of sherds that can be reassembled into a vessel, then the tag is attached to the handle of the pottery bucket containing the sherds.

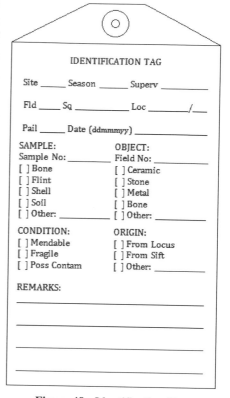

Enter the following information into the header section of this "form":

- **Site**—Enter "TeH" for Tall el-Hammam.

- **Season**—Enter the 4-digit year (e.g., "2013").

- **Superv**—Enter the Square Supervisor's first initial and last name.

- **Fld**—Enter the 2-letter combination of Tall (**U**pper or **L**ower) and Field (e.g., "LA").

- **Sq**—Enter the Square number (e.g., "42K").

- **Loc**—Enter the Locus number.

- **Pail**—Enter the Pottery Bucket Number with which the **Object** or **Sample** is associated.

Figure 48 - Identification Tag

- **Date**—Enter the date that the **Object** or **Sample** was removed from the Locus.

> *Note: All of this information should also be entered into or is derived from the Pottery Reading Summary form (see Section 11.4).*

If the Identification Tag is used for a **Sample** taken from the Locus, enter the **Sample No** and blacken the box that best describes the material of the **Sample** (**Bone**, **Flint**, **Shell**, **Soil**, or **Other**). If **Other** is blackened, explain here or in the **Remarks** section if more space is needed.

If the Identification Tag is used for an **Object** taken from the Locus, enter the **Object** number in **Field No** and blacken the box that best describes the material of the **Object** (**Ceramic**, **Stone**, **Metal**, **Bone**, or **Other**). If **Other** is blackened, explain here or in the **Remarks** section if more space is needed. (Note: A rubber stamp is used to make Identification Tags out of plain manila stock tags. The rubber stamp erroneously contains

"Field" instead of "Object" and it is easier to reprogram our brains than to fix or replace the stamp.)

Blacken the box that best describes the **Condition** of the **Object** or **Sample**. The options are:

- ☐ **Mendable**—It can be fixed or reassembled.
- ☐ **Fragile**—Whether whole or in pieces, the **Object** or **Sample** can be broken easily. Handle with care!
- ☐ **Poss Contam**—The **Sample** or **Object** (if in pieces) is possibly contaminated with material or other pieces that do not belong to it.

Blacken the box that best describes the **Origin** of the **Object** or **Sample**. The options are:

- ☐ **From Locus**—The **Object** or **Sample** was discovered in and removed directly from the Locus during excavation.
- ☐ **From Sift**— The **Object** or **Sample** was discovered in the sifter while screening dirt taken from the Locus during excavation.
- ☐ **Other**—Explain here or in the **Remarks** section if more space is needed.

Write any other information that might be helpful to those who will analyze the **Object** or **Sample** in the **Remarks** section.

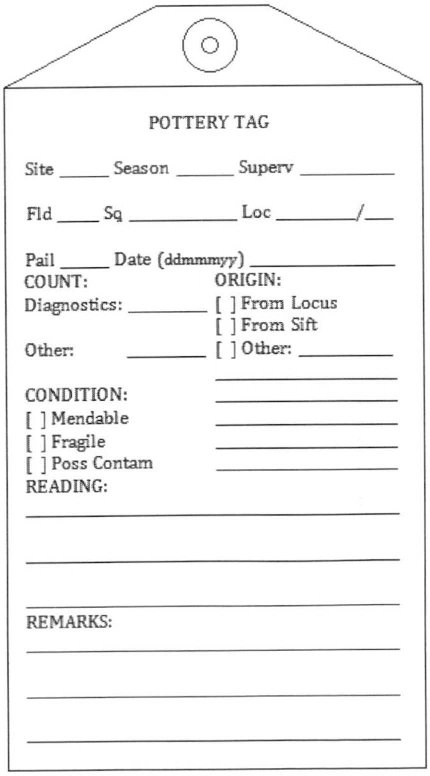
POTTERY TAG

Site ____ Season _____ Superv ________

Fld ____ Sq _________ Loc ______/___

Pail ____ Date (ddmmmyy) __________

COUNT:
Diagnostics: ______
Other: ______

ORIGIN:
[ ] From Locus
[ ] From Sift
[ ] Other: _______

CONDITION:
[ ] Mendable
[ ] Fragile
[ ] Poss Contam

READING:

REMARKS:

Figure 49 - Pottery Tag

11.12 Pottery Tag

The Pottery Tag, shown in Figure 49, is attached to each Pottery Bucket that is used to collect sherds excavated from a Locus. If the pottery bucket contains sherds that are believed to be from a single vessel, then it may be used as an Identification Tag (see Section 11.11) with "OBJECT: SINGLE VESSEL" written boldly (all cap's) into the **Remarks** section.

The header section of the Pottery Tag is identical to the header section of the Identification Tag (see Section 11.11).

Enter the number of **Diagnostics** (diagnostic sherds) and non-diagnostic (**Other**) in the **Count** section of the Pottery Tag.

The **Origin** section of the Pottery Tag is identical to the **Origin** section of the Identification Tag (see Section 11.11). Note, however, that this section of the Pottery Tag is usually left blank unless the Pottery Bucket contains the sherds from a single vessel, in which case you should blacken the appropriate box. Most sherds in the Pottery

Bucket are removed directly from the Square. Some, however, are found in the sifter during screening of the dirt from the Square, but no distinction is made in the general collection of sherds placed in the Pottery Bucket.

The **Condition** section of the Pottery Tag is identical to the **Condition** section of the Identification Tag (see Section 11.11). Once again, this section of the Pottery Tag is usually left blank unless the Pottery Bucket contains the sherds from a single vessel. (All sherds are considered to be fragile.)

Leave the **Reading** section of the Pottery Tag blank. The Pottery Tag is given to the Object Registrar at Pottery Reading, and this section is completed by the Pottery Registrar at that time.

Write any other information that might be helpful to those who will analyze the pottery sherds in the **Remarks** section.

11.13 Pottery Reading Record [PR^2]

Starting in Season Nine (2014), pottery processing (counting, soaking, washing, and drying) is handled by a team of volunteers on site at Tall el-Hammam. The dried sherds are transported to the dig hotel for reading by senior staff on a weekly (more or less) basis.

The Pottery Reading Record (see Figure 50) is used at the pottery reading to record the reading results. This form is filled out by either the Square Supervisor (if present) or a volunteer "scribe."

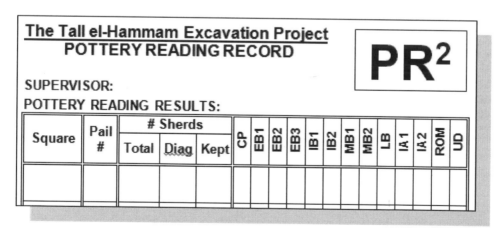

Figure 50 - Pottery Reading Record

The protocol typically used at pottery reading is to read all of the pottery by Supervisor, as identified from the Pottery Tag (see Section 11.12). Hence, the Supervisor's name is entered in the designated space at the top of the form. The **Square** Code and **Pail #** are transcribed from the Pottery Tag to uniquely identify the pottery being read. This information is later used by the Supervisor to transcribe the pottery reading results to the appropriate Pottery Reading Summary (see Section 11.4). The **Total** and **Diag**nostic number of sherds is also transcribed from the Pottery Tag.

As the sherds are read, a running total of sherds kept and registered is entered by archaeological period (**CP**, **EB1**, **EB2**, etc.). If the assemblage of sherds yields none kept, then an "X" may be placed in the appropriate box(es) to indicate the archaeological period(s) that the readers identify in the assemblage of sherds.

The total number of diagnostic sherds that are **Kept** and registered is entered after the contents of the drying basket are read.

> *Note: It is the responsibility of each Square Supervisor to retrieve their completed Pottery Reading Record forms and transcribe the information to the Pottery Reading Summary forms.*

The Pottery Reading Record forms are double-sided (same on both sides). After transcribing the information to the Pottery Reading Summary forms, draw crossing diagonal lines from corner-to-corner to mark that side of the form as having been transcribed. If the opposite side of the form is still unused, then return it to the pottery room for use at a subsequent pottery reading. If both sides of the form have been used, then toss it in the trash.

11.14 Level Calculation Form [LC]

The Level Calculation Form may be used to assist with measuring levels within a Square. Space is provided to perform the needed calculations and record the locations within the Square where the levels are measured.

> *Note: The Level Calculation Form is optional and does not have to be submitted with your paperwork at the end of the Season. It is intended to help you calculate levels more accurately and provide a cross-check for the numbers that you enter into your Locus forms.*

Referring to Figure 51, enter the **Date** on which the level is measured, the **Square Code** in which the level is measured, and the **Locus #** for which the level is measured. Also enter whether the measurement is for an opening or closing level (enter "O" or "C", respectively, in **Open/Close**.) Also, using the **Locus and Level Locations** grid on the Locus forms (see Figure 52), enter the grid cell number where the level is measured into **Loc**.

Date (ddmmmyy)	Square Code (Area/Field/Square)	Locus #	Bench Mark Level 1.	+	A 2.	=	String Level 3.	−	B 4.	=	Final Level 5.	Open/ Close*	Loc.

Figure 51 - [LC] Level Calculations

Locus and Level Locations					
1	2	3	4	5	6
7	8	9	10	11	12
13	14	15	16	17	18
19	20	21	22	23	24
25	26	27	28	29	30
31	32	33	34	35	36

Figure 52 - [LC] Locus and Level Locations

Note: The string that you use for measuring levels must be secured to a stake that is less than two Squares away from the nearest Bench Mark. The string must also be able to sweep the entire locus without hitting any obstructions. (You may also tie the string to the Bench Mark stake itself if it is located in the same or an adjacent Square.)

Use the center section of the Level Calculation Form to do the actual calculation. Use the 6-step process described below to calculate a level when the string used for measuring the level is above the Bench Mark, as shown in Figure 53.

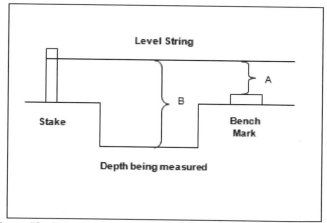

Figure 53 - [LC] Calculating Levels with String above Bench Mark

Step 1. Enter the **Bench Mark Level**. (Remember that all levels at Tall el-Hammam are negative numbers because the Site in <u>below sea level</u>.)

Step 2. Measure and enter the height of the string (**A**) above the Bench Mark. (It does not matter if the string is tied to a Bench Mark stake or a separate stake as shown in Figure 52.)

74

Step 3.   Calculate the **String Level** by adding measurement **A** to the **Bench Mark Level**. (The sum should be a smaller negative number than the **Bench Mark Level** itself because the string is less below sea level than the Bench Mark. It it's not, you did the arithmetic incorrectly. Try again!)

Step 4.   Measure and enter the height of the string (**B**) above the desired location in the Locus.

Step 5.   Calculate the **Final Level** by subtracting **B** from the **String Level**. (The sum should be a larger negative number than the **Bench Mark Level** itself because the measured level is further below sea level than the Bench Mark. It it's not, you did the arithmetic incorrectly. Try again!)

Step 6.   Copy the **Final Level** to the Locus form.

If the string level is the same as the Bench Mark Level, as shown in Figure 54, use an abbreviated 4-step process by simply skipping over steps 2 and 3, above. In other words, do Step 5 by subtracting **B** directly from the **Bench Mark Level**.

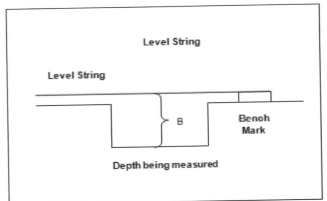

Figure 54 - [LC] Calculating Levels with String at Bench Mark Level

Note: If you do not have a "primary" Bench Mark in your area to use as a starting point, you can pick your own location for a Bench Mark (see Section 11.3) and still do steps 2 and 4, postponing the other steps until after you get the actual Bench Mark Level from the Site Surveyor. This will become your "Primary" Bench Mark for the remainder of the Season.

12 DRAWINGS

Square Supervisors will perform all Locus, Balk, and Square Drawings.

12.1 Locus Top Plan Drawings

A top plan should be drawn, in pencil, for each Locus **except Locus #1.** There is no need to draw Locus #1 as this is the 5cm surface soil. However, its top and bottom elevation levels should be included on the top plan for Locus #2. Every top plan should have the level listed as "T" for top/opening and underneath it "B" for bottom/closing. Remember at Tall el-Hammam the elevation is a negative number as we are below Sea Level., thus the bottom levels should be larger negative numbers than the top levels. Record this at the location the level was taken. In addition, all plans should include any object(s) found and its location and bottom level.

All drawings should be oriented so that "North" is at the top of the graph paper. The drawing should be a fair representation of the Locus. First draw the outline of the Square and its North and East Balks. Sketch any stones, mudbricks, or special features with a single line. Describe the Locus under the remarks section on the graph paper (see Figure 55, below).

12.2 Square Top Drawing

At various times throughout the Season, draw an overall top plan of the Square with all "open" Loci and record the Locus numbers in their specific locations.

Before closing your Square (whether moving to a new Square or departing for the Season), draw a final Square top plan (see Figure 56, below).

12.3 Balk Drawings

Balk drawings should be drawn a couple of days prior to closing the Square (whether you are moving to a new Square or departing for the Season). The balk drawings illustrate all the Loci within a Square as seen in the balk. This drawing assists the Executive Staff in the "off Season" in determining the correct strata. At the top of the graph paper, indicate the direction (N/S/E/W) that the balk is situated. Record the various levels for each Locus to the side of the drawing (see Figure 57, below).

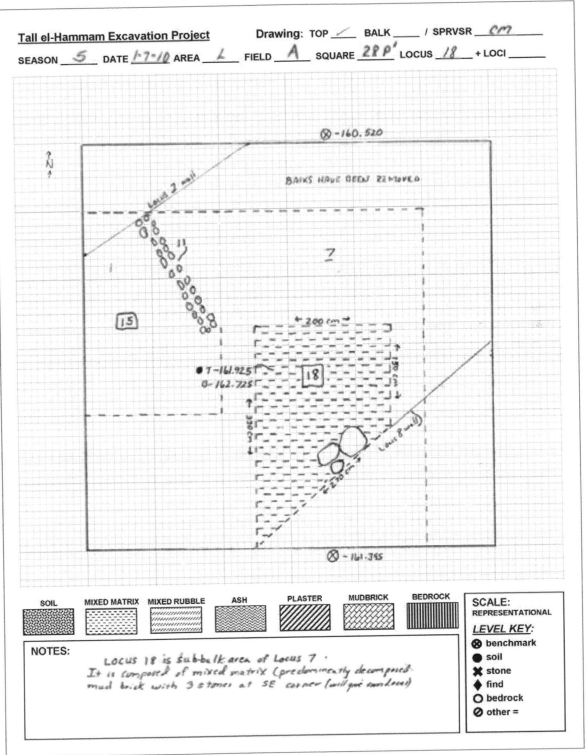

Figure 55 - Sample Square Drawing

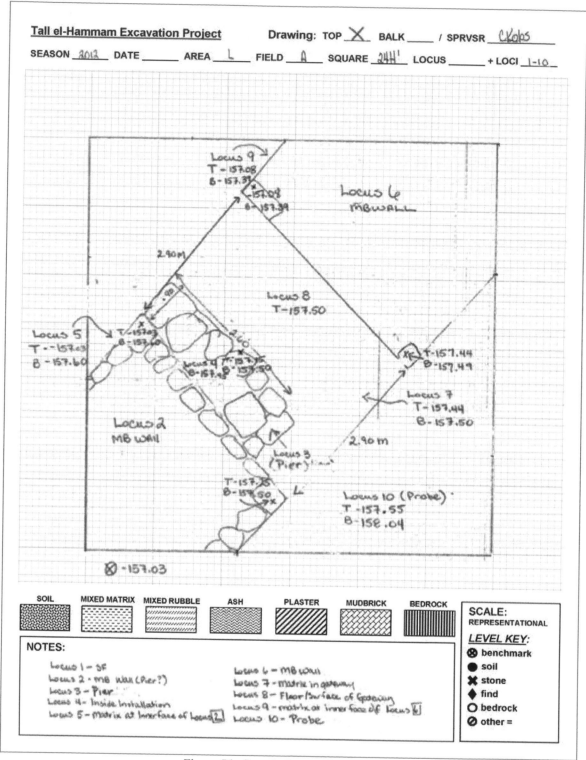

Figure 56 - Sample Square Top Drawing

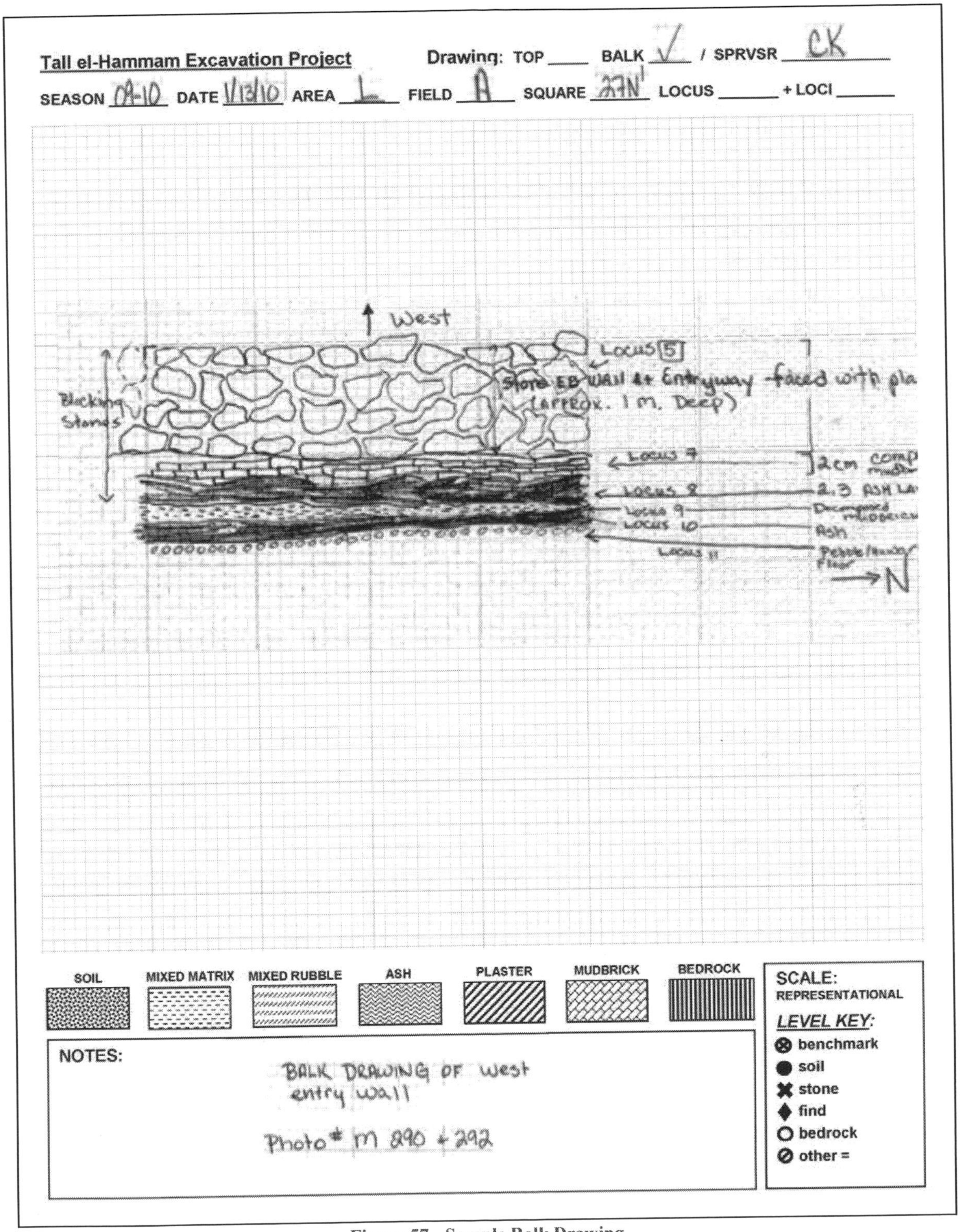

Tall el-Hammam Excavation Project Drawing: TOP _____ BALK ✓ / SPRVSR __CK__

SEASON _09-10_ DATE _1/13/10_ AREA _L_ FIELD _A_ SQUARE _27N'_ LOCUS _____ + LOCI _____

Drawing annotations:
- ↑ West
- Blocking Stones
- Locus [5]
- Stone EB Wall at Entryway - faced with pla[ster] (approx. 1 m. Deep)
- Locus 7 — 2 cm COMP[act] mud...
- Locus 8 — 2-3 ASH La...
- Locus 9 — Decomposed mudbrick...
- Locus 10 — Ash
- Locus 11 — Pebble/...Floor
- → N

Legend: SOIL | MIXED MATRIX | MIXED RUBBLE | ASH | PLASTER | MUDBRICK | BEDROCK

SCALE: REPRESENTATIONAL

LEVEL KEY:
- ⊗ benchmark
- ● soil
- ✖ stone
- ◆ find
- ○ bedrock
- ⊘ other =

NOTES:

BALK DRAWING OF WEST entry wall

Photo # m 290 + 292

Figure 57 - Sample Balk Drawing

13 GENERAL REMINDERS

- Instruct your Volunteers to leave all emerging stones or mudbricks *in situ* until you can establish a relationship. "Pedestal" these stones and mudbricks by cutting the underlying soils straight down with the trowel (do not undercut) until you are certain that nothing lies underneath them. If three or more stones or bricks are in a line, they may indicate a wall or installation (e.g., a fire pit) instead of tumble.

- Keep your balks straight and defined throughout the day. Beginning at the time specified by senior field staff, make this step part of your Square's clean-up duties. (Note: If straightening the balks is <u>not</u> done simultaneously with excavating the locus, then any artifacts, objects or sherds dislodged from the balk during cleaning must be collected in a separate pottery bucket whose Pottery Tag is marked with a "B" [Balk] for Locus.)

- A floor/surface is a good place to take a soil sample. Look closely for decomposed materials.

- The fill from an installation is a separate Locus (soil Locus) from the installation Locus itself. (Note: Changes in soil in the immediate proximity of and parallel to an Architectural Locus (i.e., a wall) may actually be a Foundation Trench Installation Locus instead of a Soil Locus.)

- Instruct your Volunteers that no object should be removed until the level and official photograph have been taken. Do not dig it out, but excavate an area surrounding it. Also, be sure to take a level reading of the lowest point of the object's location after it is removed.

- Always excavate from the known to the unknown. This helps to recognize new Loci and identify their relationships.

- Leave sherds, bones, and stones in place that protrude from the balk if they are secure.

- Do the sifting at an ample distance from your Square. If necessary, sift into a wheelbarrow and dump the dirt into a pile located far enough away that it is unlikely to be in the way of future excavation.

- Sub-balk areas in your Square when you are short on Volunteers or need to probe in specific locations.

- Instruct Volunteers not to step into any Square in which they are not working without permission. The Square may have recently been cleaned for photos or possibly an artifact is hidden by that Square's crew for a later extraction.

- Familiarize your Volunteers with Pottery and Objects and their collection methods. Pottery sherds go in a pottery bucket with a pottery tag attached. Objects (artifacts or ¾ or more of a vessel) will be put in a mesh bag with an identification tag or an identification envelope. Objects should **not** go into a pottery bucket, but be carried separately. If an object can be washed, do so in the pottery room sink. Give all objects to the Registrar at Pottery Reading.

- Pottery sherds that show signs of melting (i.e., have a glassy surface) or have an expanded matrix and feel very light (like pumice) should be treated as objects (i.e., separately bagged and tagged).

- Bone fragments should be placed in an appropriately marked manila object envelope. Larger bones will be placed in a mesh bag with an identification tag and put in the pottery room in the "bone basket". Do NOT wash bones.

- Be mindful of the time on the excavation (lunch time, breaks, and clean up).

A Senior Staff member will specify the ending time for each day's activities. About 30 minutes prior to the specified ending time, begin wrapping up by straightening balks, gathering tools, counting the pottery bucket sherds and record Diagnostics and Total Counts. You should train Volunteers to perform these tasks.

All tools and equipment should be loaded onto the truck by the specified ending time. However, Supervisor cases and pottery buckets should be hand-carried to the Mosque and NOT placed on the truck.

All Volunteers and Staff should assist with unloading the truck and storing the equipment in the Mosque storage room.

APPENDIX A—DATA COLLECTION FORMS

A total of thirteen (13) data collection forms have been developed for the Tall el-Hammam Excavation Project. These forms are divided into three different groups, as outlined below. Detailed instructions for using these forms are provided in Part Two, Section 11, of this Field Manual.

1) <u>Forms pertaining to Squares</u>. The three forms in this group are used for recording data relating to the Square as a whole rather than to individual Loci (see the next grouping, below). It is required that these three forms be initiated and maintained for each Square. A new set of forms should be used for each Season in which excavation of the Square is conducted.

   a) Locus Log **[LL]**. This form is used to maintain a sequential, enumerated listing of the Loci that are identified and excavated within the Square. The first Locus in a newly opened Square is, by definition, No. 1. Thereafter, they are numbered sequentially. The Locus Log is closed when the Square is closed or at the end of the Season, whichever comes first. If the Square is reopened in a subsequent Season, a new Locus Log is started. In this case, the number of the first Locus listed should be the next in sequence from the previously used Locus Log.

   b) Bench Mark Information **[BMI]**. This form may be used to record the level and location (relative to other known area features such as the corners of existing Squares) of bench marks used for taking level readings within a Square. "Primary" bench marks are set by the site surveyor. If they are further away than one Square from where you are taking level reading, then the accuracy of your readings will suffer due to "sag" in the line used with the string level. The Square Supervisor may establish "secondary" bench marks closer to the Square being worked whose level is derived either directly or indirectly from a "primary" bench mark. The locations and levels of all bench marks should be recorded on this form in case the bench marks are disturbed during the Season.

   c) Pottery Reading Summary **[PR]**. This form is used to maintain a sequential, enumerated listing of the pottery buckets that are used within a Square. The first pottery bucket in a newly opened Square is, by definition, No. 1. Thereafter, they are numbered sequentially regardless of which Locus it is used in. The Pottery Reading Summary is closed when the Square is closed or at the end of the Season, whichever comes first. If the Square is reopened in a subsequent Season, a new Pottery Reading Summary is started. In this case, the number of the first pottery bucket listed should be the next in sequence from the previously used Pottery Reading Summary.

   d) Weekly Supervisor Log **[WS]**. This form is used to record a weekly journal of the activities that occurred during each week that excavation is conducted in a Square. A new Weekly Supervisor Log should be completed at the end of each week.

2) Forms pertaining to Loci. The five (5) forms and two (2) tags in this group are used for recording data relating to the individual Loci within a Square. It is required that these forms be initiated and maintained for each Locus while it is being excavated.

    a) Soil Locus Form **[SL]**. This form is used to record the data pertaining to a soil Locus. A separate form should be used for each soil Locus. This form should be initiated before excavation of the soil Locus begins. The "Date Closed" should be used to record the date on which excavation of the Locus is completed (i.e., it is completely removed or excavation of the Locus is suspended for the Season), the Square itself is closed (or excavation of the Square is suspended for the Season), or the end of the Season. If the Square and Locus is reopened in a subsequent Season, a new Soil Locus Form should be used (with a new Locus number) to record the current Season's excavation activity.

    b) Architectural Locus Form **[AL]**. This form is used to record the data pertaining to an architectural Locus. A separate form should be used for each architectural Locus. This form should be initiated before excavation of the architectural Locus begins. The "Date Closed" should be used to record the date on which excavation of the Locus is completed (i.e., it is completely removed or excavation of the Locus is suspended for the Season), the Square itself is closed (or excavation of the Square is suspended for the Season), or the end of the Season. If the Square and Locus is reopened in a subsequent Season, a new Architectural Locus Form should be used (with a new Locus number) to record the current Season's excavation activity.

    c) Functional Surface Locus Form **[FSL]**. This form is used to record the data pertaining to a functional surface Locus. A separate form should be used for each functional surface Locus. This form should be initiated before excavation of the functional surface Locus begins. The "Date Closed" should be used to record the date on which excavation of the Locus is completed (i.e., it is completely removed or excavation of the Locus is suspended for the Season), the Square itself is closed (or excavation of the Square is suspended for the Season), or the end of the Season. If the Square and Locus is reopened in a subsequent Season, a new Functional Surface Locus Form should be used (with a new Locus number) to record the current Season's excavation activity.

    d) Installation Locus Form **[IL]**. This form is used to record the data pertaining to an installation Locus. A separate form should be used for each installation Locus. This form should be initiated before excavation of the installation Locus begins. The "Date Closed" should be used to record the date on which excavation of the Locus is completed (i.e., it is completely removed or excavation of the Locus is suspended for the Season), the Square itself is closed (or excavation of the Square is suspended for the Season), or the end of the Season. If the Square and Locus is reopened in a subsequent Season, a new Installation Locus Form should be used (with a new Locus number) to record the current Season's excavation activity.

e) Skeleton/Burial Locus Form **[S/BL]**. This form is used to record the data pertaining to a skeleton/burial Locus. A separate form should be used for each skeleton/burial Locus. This form should be initiated before excavation of the skeleton/burial Locus begins. The "Date Closed" should be used to record the date on which excavation of the Locus is completed (i.e., it is completely removed or excavation of the Locus is suspended for the Season), the Square itself is closed (or excavation of the Square is suspended for the Season), or the end of the Season. If the Square and Locus is reopened in a subsequent Season, a new Skeleton/Burial Locus Form should be used (with a new Locus number) to record the current Season's excavation activity.

f) Drawing Form. This form is used for creating a scaled drawing of a square to show loci, installations, objects, etc. Typically, at least one copy of the Drawing Form should accompany each Locus Form.

g) Identification Tag. This "form" is attached to each object that is excavated from a Locus. If small enough to be placed in a net bag, the tab is attached to the bag. If the "object" is a bucket full of sherds that can be reassembled into a vessel, then the tag is attached to the pottery bucket containing the sherds.

h) Pottery Tag. This "form" is attached to each pottery bucket that is used to collect sherds excavated from a Locus. If the pottery bucket contains sherds that are believed to be from a single vessel, then it may be used as an Identification Tag (see above) with "Single Vessel" written into the Remarks section.

3) Miscellaneous forms. The two (2) forms in this group are for the Square Supervisor's personal use and are not intended to be retained as a part of the permanent documentation.

a) Level Calculation Form **[LC]**. This form may be used to assist with measuring levels within a Square. Space is provided to perform the needed calculations and record the locations within the Square where the levels are measured.

b) Pottery Reading Record **[PR^2]**. This form is used at pottery readings to record the observations of the readers. The information on these forms must be transcribed by the Square Supervisors onto the corresponding Pottery Reading Summary **[PR]** forms.

The Tall el-Hammam Excavation Project
LOCUS LOG

SQUARE IDENTIFICATION:

Season	Square Code (Area/Field/Square)	Date Square Opened (ddmmmyy)	Date Square Closed (ddmmmyy)	Supervisor	Sheet
					of

LOCUS INFORMATION:

Locus #	Date Locus Opened (ddmmmyy)	Date Locus Closed (ddmmmyy)	Bucket #s	Locus Description Type*	Description	Estimated Ceramic Stratum**

*Soil, Wall, F/S (Floor/Surface), Install (Installation), Skel (Skeleton), Burial.
**To be completed by senior staff only.

86

BACK
LOCUS LOG

Season	Square Code

Sheet
of

LOCUS INFORMATION:

Locus #	Date Locus Opened (ddmmmyy)	Date Locus Closed (ddmmmyy)	Bucket #s	Locus Description		Estimated Ceramic Stratum**
				Type*	Description	

*Soil, Wall, F/S (Floor/Surface), Install (Installation), Skel (Skeleton), Burial.
**To be completed by senior staff only.

The Tall el-Hammam Excavation Project
BENCH MARK INFORMATION

Season	Square Code

Season	Supervisor	No.	Bench Mark Location References	Level
		P / S		
		P / S		
		P / S		
		P / S		
		P / S		
		P / S		
		P / S		
		P / S		
		P / S		
		P / S		
		P / S		
		P / S		
		P / S		

BACK
BENCH MARK INFORMATION

Season	Square Code

Use this symbol ⊗ to show the approximate location of each benchmark listed on the front of this form relative to the 6-meter square, which is outlined by the darker line. (Each square, below, represents one square meter.)

The Tall el-Hammam Excavation Project
POTTERY READING SUMMARY

SQUARE IDENTIFICATION:

Season	Square Code (Area/Field/Square)	Date Square Opened (ddmmmyy)	Date Square Closed (ddmmmyy)	Supervisor	Sheet
					of

POTTERY READING RESULTS:

Bucket Date (ddmmmyy)	Bucket #	Locus #	# Sherds Total	# Sherds Diag	# Sherds Kept	Reading Results

BACK
POTTERY READING SUMMARY

Season	Square Code

Sheet
of

POTTERY READING RESULTS:

Bucket Date (ddmmmyy)	Bucket #	Locus #	# Sherds			Reading Results
			Total	Diag	Kept	

The Tall el-Hammam Excavation Project
WEEKLY SUPERVISOR LOG

Season	Square Code (Area/Field/Square)	Date Week Started (ddmmmyy)	Date Week Ended (ddmmmyy)	Supervisor	Sheet
					of

Crew Members	

Date (ddmmmyy)	Locus #	Action Taken

92

BACK
WEEKLY SUPERVISOR LOG

Season	Square Code	Date Week Started (ddmmmyy)	Date Week Ended (ddmmmyy)	Sheet
				of

Comments:

_____

_____

_____

_____

_____

_____

_____

_____

_____

_____

Rough Sketch:

The Tall el-Hammam Excavation Project
SOIL LOCUS FORM

LOCUS IDENTIFICATION:

Season	Square Code (Area/Field/Square)	Locus #	Date Opened (ddmmmyy)	Date Closed (ddmmmyy)	Supervisor

TYPE OF SOIL LOCUS:

Type of Soil Locus (■ 1):	□ Surface Soil Locus	□ Cleanup Soil Locus	□ Analytical Soil Locus

REASON FOR NEW ANALYTICAL SOIL LOCUS

1. Change in Soil (■ all that apply):	□ Color	□ Texture	□ Consistency		□ Contents	□ Not Applicable
2. Diff from Previous Locus Is (■ 1):	□ Very Clear	□ Clear	□ Somewhat Clear	□ Arbitrary	□ Not Applicable

SOIL COMPOSTION:

Soil Level* (■ 1)	Soil Color (Use Munsell Soil Color Charts) Color Code	Color Name	Soil Texture (■ one)	Soil Consistency (■ one)	Soil Contents (■ all that apply) (Explain All "Others" in Notes)
□P □S □T			□Silty/Loamy □Clayey □Sandy □Ashy	□Loose □Crushable □Hard	**ARTIFACTS:** □Pottery □Bone □Shell □Glass □Metal □Lithic □Organic □Other **ARCHITECTURAL DEBRIS** (fallen or out of place): □Mudbrick □Wall-Stone □Other
□P □S □T			□Silty/Loamy □Clayey □Sandy □Ashy	□Loose □Crushable □Hard	**NON-ARCHITECTURAL ROCKS:** □Pebbles □Cobbles □Stones □Boulders **BURNED MATERIAL:** □Ash □Charcoal □Other
□P □S □T			□Silty/Loamy □Clayey □Sandy □Ashy	□Loose □Crushable □Hard	**MODERN MATERIAL:** □No □Yes _____ **OTHER:** _____

*P = primary (dominant) soil, S = secondary (next dominant) soil, T = tertiary (least dominant) soil. Mudbrick is not a soil.

LOCUS LEVELS: **LOCUS LOCATION:**   **LOCUS RELATIONSHIPS:**

Loc. Code*	Opening (Top)	Closing (Bottom)	Diff.	Locus and Level Locations						Relation-ships	Locus or Square/Locus #s**
				1	2	3	4	5	6	Under	
				7	8	9	10	11	12	Over	
				13	14	15	16	17	18	Abuts	
				19	20	21	22	23	24	Equals	
				25	26	27	28	29	30	Cuts	
				31	32	33	34	35	36	Cut By	

*Location Code—Use codes 1-36 to show the location of the levels. **Use square/locus #s under "Equals" if the locus is in a different square.

NOTES

_____

_____

_____

_____

_____

_____

BACK
SOIL LOCUS FORM

Season	Square Code	Locus #

BUCKET CONTENTS:

Date (ddmmmyy)	Bucket #	General #s		Special Objects (Significant Artifacts)		
		# Sherds	# Bones	Object Description	# Items	Elevation (at lowest point)

PHOTOGRAPHS:

Date (ddmmmyy)	Photo #	Direction*	Subject

*The direction the photographer faced when taking the picture (N, S, E, W, NW, NE, SW, SE, or DOWN (i.e., straight down on an artifact)).

SAMPLES (Show date(s) each sample was collected in ddmmmyy format)

Dry Soil	Water-Screening	Flotation	Radiocarbon	Other_____

STRATIGRAPHIC ANALYSIS (Completed by senior staff only)

Stratum			Interpretation/Comments
Period	Sub-Period	Phase	

The Tall el-Hammam Excavation Project
ARCHITECTURAL LOCUS FORM

LOCUS IDENTIFICATION:

Season	Square Code (Area/Field/Square)	Locus #	Date Opened (ddmmmyy)	Date Closed (ddmmmyy)	Supervisor

WALL CONSTRUCTION:

Material	Construction Style	Dominant Size	Mortar	Wall Finish ↓Inside Outside↓	Mudbrick Composition
□ Mudbrick	□ Head/Stretch □ Stacked □ Tied □ Other	(cm) L:_____ W:_____ T:_____	□ None (Dry) □ Mud/Clay □ Mud/Clay/Ash □ Other	□ Mud/Clay □ □ Plaster □ □ Other □ □ Unknown □	Main Ingredient: □ Mud □ Clay □ Huwar □ Other
□ Masonry □ Unworked Fieldstones □ Worked Fieldstones	□ Chinked □ Rubble-Filled □ Rubble □ Other	% ___Cobbles (7.6-24.9 cm) ___Stones (25.0-59.9 cm) ___Boulders (60.0+ cm)	□ None (Dry) □ Mud/Clay □ Mud/Clay/Ash □ Other	□ None □ □ Mud/Clay □ □ Mud/Clay/Ash □ □ Plaster □ □ Other □	Temper/Binder: □ Straw □ Pottery Sherds □ Pebbles □ Other □ Unknown
□ Dressed/ Ashlar Blocks	□ Head/Stretch □ Orthostat □ Quoin & Pier □ Rubble-Filled □ Other	(cm) L:_____ W:_____ T:_____	□ None (Dry) □ Mud/Clay □ Cement □ Other	□ None □ □ Plaster □ □ Other □	Munsell Color Code: _____ Munsell Description: _____

ARCHITECTURAL LOCUS RELATIONSHIPS

Relationship	Locus # or Square/Locus #
Bonding Walls	
Abutting Walls	
Foundation Wall	
Superstructure Wall	
Foundation Trench	
Associated FL/Surf.	
Extends into Abutting Square(s) as Locus(i)*	

NON-ARCHITECTURAL LOCUS RELATIONSHIPS

Relationship	Locus Numbers
Under	
Over	
Abuts	
Cuts	
Cut By	

*Use both the Square / Locus #. If the locus # is not yet known in the abutting square, then use "?" as the locus #.

LOCUS LEVELS:

Loc. Code*	Opening (Top)	Closing (Bottom)	Diff.

LOCUS LOCATION:

Locus and Level Locations

1	2	3	4	5	6
7	8	9	10	11	12
13	14	15	16	17	18
19	20	21	22	23	24
25	26	27	28	29	30
31	32	33	34	35	36

OVERALL WALL SIZE:

Dimension	Size
Length (m) (within square)	
Thickness (cm)	Max: Min:
Height (cm)	Max: Min:
# of Existing Courses (i.e., # rows high)	Max: Min: □ Cannot Be Determined

*Location Code—Use codes 1-36 to show the general locations where the levels were taken.

96

BACK
ARCHITECTURAL LOCUS FORM

Season	Square Code	Locus #

NOTES:

_____

_____

_____

_____

_____

_____

BUCKET CONTENTS:

Date (ddmmmyy)	Bucket #	General #s		Specific Objects (Significant Artifacts)		
		# Sherds	# Bones	Object Description	# Items	Elevation (at lowest point)

PHOTOGRAPHS:

Date (ddmmmyy)	Photo #	Direction*	Subject

*The direction the photographer faced when taking the picture (N, S, E, W, NW, NE, SW, SE).

SAMPLES (Show date(s) each sample was collected in ddmmmyy format)

Dry Soil Sample	Waterscreening	Flotation	Radiocarbon	Other_____

STRATIGRAPHIC ANALYSIS (Completed by senior staff only)

Stratum			Interpretation/Comments	Structure #	Wall #
Period	Sub-Period	Phase			

The Tall el-Hammam Excavation Project
FUNCTIONAL SURFACE LOCUS FORM

LOCUS IDENTIFICATION:

Season	Square Code (Area/Field/Square)	Locus #	Date Opened (ddmmmyy)	Date Closed (ddmmmyy)	Supervisor

REASON FOR NEW FUNCTIONAL SURFACE LOCUS

1. Change in Soil (■ all that apply):	□ Color	□ Texture	□ Consistency	□ Contents	□ Not Applicable
2. Diff from Previous Locus Is (■ 1):	□ Very Clear	□ Clear	□ Somewhat Clear	□ Arbitrary	□ Not Applicable

FUNCTIONAL SURFACE MATERIAL AND CHARACTERISTICS (■ all that apply):

Material	Dominant Size	Munsell Color Code	Munsell Description
□ Beaten Earth	XXXXXXXXXXXXXXXXXXXX		
□ Lime	XXXXXXXXXXXXXXXXXXXX		
□ Plaster	XXXXXXXXXXXXXXXXXXXX		
□ Huwar	XXXXXXXXXXXXXXXXXXXX		
□ Mudbrick	L: W: T: cm		
□ Baked Brick	L: W: T: cm		
□ Tessera (Mosaic)	L: W: T: cm		
□ Crushed Rock/Pebbles	(<=7.5 cm) _____ %	XXXXXXXXXX	XXXXXXXXXXXXXXXXXXX
□ Cobble	(7.6-24.9 cm) _____ %	XXXXXXXXXX	XXXXXXXXXXXXXXXXXXX
□ Stone	(25.0-59.9 cm) _____ %	XXXXXXXXXX	XXXXXXXXXXXXXXXXXXX
□ Boulder	(60.0+ cm) _____ %	XXXXXXXXXX	XXXXXXXXXXXXXXXXXXX
□ Other:			

LOCUS LEVELS: **LOCUS LOCATION:**   **LOCUS RELATIONSHIPS:**

Loc. Code*	Opening (Top)	Closing (Bottom)	Diff.	Locus and Level Locations						Relation- ships	Locus or Square/Locus #s**
				1	2	3	4	5	6	Under	
				7	8	9	10	11	12	Over	
				13	14	15	16	17	18	Abuts	
				19	20	21	22	23	24	Equals	
				25	26	27	28	29	30	Cuts	
				31	32	33	34	35	36	Cut By	

*Location Code—Use codes 1-36 to show the location of the levels. **Use square/locus #s under "Equals" if the locus is in a different square.

NOTES:

_____

_____

_____

_____

_____

_____

BACK
FUNCTIONAL SURFACE LOCUS FORM

Season	Square Code	Locus #

BUCKET CONTENTS:

Date (ddmmmyy)	Bucket #	General #s		Special Objects (Significant Artifacts)		
		# Sherds	# Bones	Object Description	# Items	Elevation (at lowest point)

PHOTOGRAPHS:

Date (ddmmmyy)	Photo #	Direction*	Subject

*The direction the photographer faced when taking the picture (N, S, E, W, NW, NE, SW, SE, or DOWN (i.e., straight down on an artifact)).

SAMPLES (Show date(s) each sample was collected in ddmmmyy format)

Dry Soil	Water-Screening	Flotation	Radiocarbon	Other_____

STRATIGRAPHIC ANALYSIS (Completed by senior staff only)

Stratum			Interpretation/Comments
Period	Sub-Period	Phase	

The Tall el-Hammam Excavation Project
INSTALLATION LOCUS FORM

LOCUS IDENTIFICATION:

Season	Square Code (Area/Field/Square)	Locus #	Date Opened (ddmmmyy)	Date Closed (ddmmmyy)	Supervisor

TYPE OF INSTALLATION

□ Pit	□ Silo	□ Kiln	□ Tabun	□ Cistern	□ Foundation Trench	□ Other

INSTALLATION CHARACTERISTICS (■ all that apply):

MATERIAL	SHAPE	MEASUREMENTS
□ Beaten Earth	□ Linear	
□ Lime	□ Curvilinear	Length (greatest)
□ Plaster	□ Rectangular	Width (greatest)
□ Huwar	□ Triangular	or Thickness (average)
□ Mudbrick	□ Circular	Height
□ Baked Brick	□ Semi-Circular	Orientation of long axis:
□ Tessera	□ Oval	□ N □ NE □ E □ SE
□ Crushed Pebbles	□ Irregular	□ S □ SW □ W □ NW
□ Cobble	□ Other:	□ n/a (circular only)
□ Stone		
□ Boulder		
□ Other:		

LOCUS LEVELS: **LOCUS LOCATION:** **LOCUS RELATIONSHIPS:**

Loc. Code*	Opening (Top)	Closing (Bottom)	Diff.	Locus and Level Locations						Relation-ships	Locus or Square/Locus #s**
				1	2	3	4	5	6	Under	
				7	8	9	10	11	12	Over	
				13	14	15	16	17	18	Abuts	
				19	20	21	22	23	24	Equals	
				25	26	27	28	29	30	Cuts	
				31	32	33	34	35	36	Cut By	

*Location Code—Use codes 1-36 to show the location of the levels. **Use square/locus #s under "Equals" if the locus is in a different square.

NOTES

_____

_____

_____

_____

_____

_____

_____

Season	Square Code	Locus #

BUCKET CONTENTS:

Date (ddmmmyy)	Bucket #	General #s		Special Objects (Significant Artifacts)		
		# Sherds	# Bones	Object Description	# Items	Elevation (at lowest point)

PHOTOGRAPHS:

Date (ddmmmyy)	Photo #	Direction*	Subject

*The direction the photographer faced when taking the picture (N, S, E, W, NW, NE, SW, SE, or DOWN (i.e., straight down on an artifact)).

SAMPLES (Show date(s) each sample was collected in ddmmmyy format)

Dry Soil	Water-Screening	Flotation	Radiocarbon	Other_____

STRATIGRAPHIC ANALYSIS (Completed by senior staff only)

Stratum			Interpretation/Comments
Period	Sub-Period	Phase	

The Tall el-Hammam Excavation Project
SKELETON/BURIAL LOCUS FORM

LOCUS IDENTIFICATION:

Season	Square Code (Area/Field/Square)	Locus #	Date Opened (ddmmmyy)	Date Closed (ddmmmyy)	Supervisor

□ BURIAL	□ SKELETON (NON-BURIAL)

CONTAINER (if Burial):

□ Unlined Pit	□ Stone-lined Pit	□ Tomb	□ Ossuary	□ Jar	□ Sarcophagus
□ Other:					

SPECIAL CHARACTERISTICS (■ all that apply):

ACCESSIBILITY	DISPOSAL	ARTICULATION
□ Totally in Square	□ Primary Inhumation	□ Completely Articulated
□ Head in _____ Balk	□ Secondary Inhumation	□ Articulated
□ Upper Half in _____ Balk	□ Cremation	□ Semi-Articulated
□ Lower Half in _____ Balk	□ Multiple Burials	□ Disarticulated
□ Lower Legs in _____ Balk	Total Burials:	□ Completely Disarticulated
□ Other:	□ Other:	□ Fragments Only

STATISTICS:	BODY POSITION:	ORIENTATION (FACING):	
Est. Age:	□ Extended	□ North	□ South
Sex:	□ Loosely Flexed	□ East	□ West
	□ Tightly Flexed	□ Up	□ Down
	□ Unknown		

LOCUS LEVELS: **LOCUS LOCATION:**   **LOCUS RELATIONSHIPS:**

Loc. Code*	Opening (Top)	Closing (Bottom)	Diff.	Locus and Level Locations						Relation-ships	Locus or Square/Locus #s**
				1	2	3	4	5	6	Under	
				7	8	9	10	11	12	Over	
				13	14	15	16	17	18	Abuts	
				19	20	21	22	23	24	Equals	
				25	26	27	28	29	30	Cuts	
				31	32	33	34	35	36	Cut By	

*Location Code—Use codes 1-36 to show the location of the levels. **Use square/locus #s under "Equals" if the locus is in a different square.

102

Season	Square Code	Locus #

NOTES

_____

_____

_____

_____

_____

_____

BUCKET CONTENTS:

Date (ddmmmyy)	Bucket #	General #s		Special Objects (Significant Artifacts)		
		# Sherds	# Bones	Object Description	# Items	Elevation (at lowest point)

PHOTOGRAPHS:

Date (ddmmmyy)	Photo #	Direction*	Subject

*The direction the photographer faced when taking the picture (N, S, E, W, NW, NE, SW, SE, or DOWN (i.e., straight down on an artifact)).

STRATIGRAPHIC ANALYSIS (Completed by senior staff only)

Stratum			Interpretation/Comments
Period	Sub-Period	Phase	

Tall el-Hammam Excavation Project   Drawing: TOP _____ BALK _____ / SPRVSR _____

SEASON _____ DATE _____ AREA _____ FIELD _____ SQUARE _____ LOCUS _____ + LOCI _____

SOIL   MIXED MATRIX   MIXED RUBBLE   ASH   PLASTER   MUDBRICK   BEDROCK

SCALE:
REPRESENTATIONAL

LEVEL KEY:
⊗ benchmark
● soil
✖ stone
◆ find
○ bedrock
⊘ other =

NOTES:

IDENTIFICATION TAG

Site _____ Season _____ Superv _____

Fld _____ Sq _____ Loc _____/____

Pail _____ Date (ddmmmyy) _____

SAMPLE:	OBJECT:
Sample No: _____	Field No: _____
[ ] Bone	[ ] Ceramic
[ ] Flint	[ ] Stone
[ ] Shell	[ ] Metal
[ ] Soil	[ ] Bone
[ ] Other: _____	[ ] Other: _____

CONDITION:	ORIGIN:
[ ] Mendable	[ ] From Locus
[ ] Fragile	[ ] From Sift
[ ] Poss Contam	[ ] Other: _____

REMARKS:

_____

_____

_____

_____

POTTERY TAG

Site _____ Season _____ Superv _____

Fld _____ Sq _____ Loc _____/____

Pail _____ Date (ddmmmyy) _____

COUNT:	ORIGIN:
Diagnostics: _____	[ ] From Locus
	[ ] From Sift
Other: _____	[ ] Other: _____

CONDITION:
[ ] Mendable
[ ] Fragile
[ ] Poss Contam
READING:

_____

_____

_____

REMARKS:

_____

_____

_____

The Tall el-Hammam Excavation Projection
LEVEL CALCULATION FORM

NOTES:
1. If the leveL string is tied to a stake and is above the bench mark, then include steps 2 and 3 in the formula.
2. If the level string is on the bench mark, then do not include steps 2 and 3 in the formula.
3. TeH is *below* sea level, so all elevations below the bench mark move away from zero (sea level).

Date (ddmmmyy)	Square Code (Area/Field/Square)	Locus #	Bench Mark Level 1.	+	A 2.	=	String Level 3.	−	B 4.	=	Final Level 5.	Open/ Close*	Loc.

* Opening (O) or closing (C) level

Page _____ of _____

106

Method for calculating levels if the level string is above the Bench Mark.

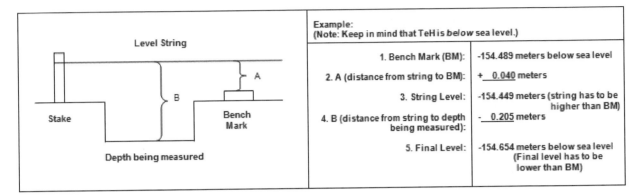

	Example: (Note: Keep in mind that TeH is *below* sea level.)
1. Bench Mark (BM):	-154.489 meters below sea level
2. A (distance from string to BM):	+__0.040 meters
3. String Level:	-154.449 meters (string has to be higher than BM)
4. B (distance from string to depth being measured):	-__0.205 meters
5. Final Level:	-154.654 meters below sea level (Final level has to be lower than BM)

Method for calculating levels if the level string is on the Bench Mark.

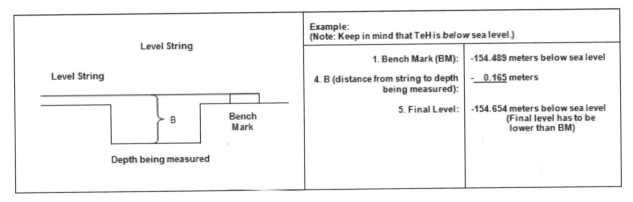

	Example: (Note: Keep in mind that TeH is *below* sea level.)
1. Bench Mark (BM):	-154.489 meters below sea level
4. B (distance from string to depth being measured):	-__0.165 meters
5. Final Level:	-154.654 meters below sea level (Final level has to be lower than BM)

The Tall el-Hammam Excavation Project
POTTERY READING RECORD

PR²

SUPERVISOR:

POTTERY READING RESULTS:

Square	Pail #	# Sherds			CP	EB1	EB2	EB3	IB1	IB2	MB1	MB2	LB	IA 1	IA2	ROM	UD
		Total	Diag	Kept													

APPENDIX B—ARCHAEOLOGY GLOSSARY

A

Age—An archaeological era, often divided into periods. It generally derives its name from the dominant technological capability of the time; for example: Lithic (stone), Chalcolithic (copper-stone), Bronze, Iron.

Amphora(e)/Amphoriskos—Greek term for a large jar with two handles.

Amulet—Small object used for personal cultic purposes.

Analytical Sherds—See *Diagnostoc Sherds*.

Apse—A semi-circular area at the east end of Byzantine churches, with a vaulted ceiling.

Aqueduct—Water channel.

Architext—The specialist who is responsible for drawing final top plans for all architecture.

Artifact—Anything that has been made or modified by humans.

Artifact Registration—The process during which artifacts are cleaned, numbered and described. A staff specialist is assigned to oversee this process.

Ashlar—Well chiseled and squared building stones.

Assemblage—A group of objects of different types found in association with each other.

B

Balk—The vertical section of earth, usually one meter wide, left between excavated squares for control of stratigraphy (standing balk). The term is also used to refer to one of the four sides of a square. Then excavating a probe, the standing balks are called *main balks* and the new, temporary balks are called *subsidiary balks*.

Balk Stamp—A rubber stamp used on balk drawings which provides space to record site, season, square, Locus, date, balk, supervisor, north (orientation), and scale.

Balk Stub—The intersection of two balks, revealed when one balk is removed.

Beaker—A pottery drinking vessel usually with a depth greater than the diameter and also usually with handles.

Beaten Earth—A hard earth surface which has been compacted by traffic. It is often associated with paths, floors, or other occupational surfaces (cf. *terre pisee*)

Bedrock—Solid underlying rock formation below the level of human activity and artifacts.

Bedrock Party—A traditional celebration marking the completion of excavation in a square. (Actually, it is merely an excuse to justify a party...almost any "reason" will do!)

Bema—A platform in a cult center.

Bench Mark—A point (usually with exact elevation in meters and centimeters above sea level—below sea level at Tall el-Hammam) to which all elevations are referenced. Also called *datum mark* or simply, *datum*.

Biodata—Organic samples (seeds, microflora, etc) collected by excavation, sifting, and flotation.

Bioturbation—Mixing of debris caused by borrowing animals.

Body Sherds—Sherds from an undiagnostic portion of a vessel.

Bone Bag—The plastic mesh bag in which bones are collected during routine excavation. Comparable to a pottery bucket for pottery.

Bonded—Two walls with interlocking stones or bricks (as opposed to abutting one another); a technique which suggests that the walls were built together at the same time.

Bossed Stone—A stone with its edge or border trimmed, leaving a rough face at the center.

Bulla(e)—Small clay object used to seal ancient documents; Iron Age examples often contain seal impressions.

Burnish—A polish given to a pottery vessel by rubbing the dried clay with a tool before firing.

C

Cairn—A mound of stones covering a burial or serving as a landmark.

Carination—Angular ridge around the body of a pottery vessel where the body takes a sharp turn.

Cartouche—Oval frame encircling an Egyptian royal name in hieroglyphic signs.

Casement Wall—A fortification system made up of two parallel walls with periodic crosswalls; in plan, it looks like a ladder.

Ceramic Technician—The specialist responsible for analyzing how pottery is made: type and mixture of clay, inclusions, firing procedures, construction techniques, initial and secondary pottery use, etc.

Characteristic Sherds—See *Diagnostic Sherds*.

Cistern—An underground pit, often plaster-lined, used for water storage. It may be associated with a system of channels for channeling water to its mouth.

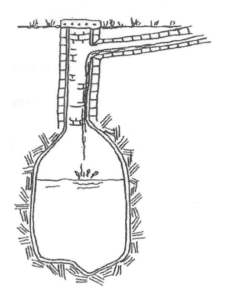

Contamination—The invasion of non-contemporaneous foreign material into a Locus or a group of finds. A Locus could have been contaminated in antiquity or by faulty excavation process.

Coprolite—Dried or fossilized feces.

Corbelling—The roof-building technique wherein stones or bricks extend over space, overlapping each other, until they meet and are then covered with a capstone.

Course—Layers of brick or stone in a wall; a stone wall, three stones high, would have three courses.

Crater—See *Krater*.

Cyclopean Wall—Wall of massive stones; irregular and close-fitting. The stones are so huge that, as the ancient Greeks said, "None but the Cyclops could have built the wall!"

Cylinder Seal—A cylinder-shaped object (most often of stone) incised to produce a seal impression when rolled over moist clay.

D

Data Processor—The staff member responsible for inputting handwritten excavation data into the computerized database.

Datum—See *Bench Mark*.

Datum Line—Fixed line in a balk with a known level. It is used for drawing to scale.

Debitage—Bits and pieces left over from a manufacturing process; e.g., "flint debitage" is the flint flakes left over from tool-making.

Detritus—Debris composed of loose, disintegrated rock and mudbrick.

Diagnostic Sherds—Sherds from rims, bases, and handles; or with decoration or special form. They are used a chronological indicators or to provide insights into the pottery-making industry.

Dipinto—A painted inscription.

Dolmen—A megalithic burial above ground level made up of two or more upright stones (set on end or edge) with a capstone.

Door-jamb—Frame of a door opening, the vertical edge of a doorway.

E

Earth Layer—A homogeneous deposit or earth that can be separated from other layers above and below.

Elevation—A drawing of a wall face. It is not the level of a feature above/below sea level. (See *Level*.)

F

Faience—Powdered quartz, covered with glaze; used primarily for Egyptian(-style) amulets and figurines.

Favissa(e)—See *Votive Deposit*.

Fibula(e)—A decorative "safety pin" used to hold clothing in place; it is usually made of bronze, rarely of bone.

Field—A sector or area of excavation made of a group of squares, and is identified by a capital Letter (e.g., Field A). Excavation is supervised by an experienced archaeologist called a Field Supervisor.

Field Notebook—The Field Notebook includes the Handbook, Introduction page, Locus sheets, supplementary sheets, top plans, and daily and weekly Summaries.

Figurine—A small model of a human or animal.

Fill—Debris used to level or elevate an area for subsequent construction activities.

Flint—Very hard stone, often used as raw material for making tools; cf. *Debitage*.

Formator—The pottery reconstructor.

Foundation Trench—A trench dug as part of a wall construction into which the foundation for the wall is laid. Archaeologically, it is treated as a pit.

Founding Level—The bottom level of a wall's foundation.

Fresco—Painting on wet plaster; a type of wall decoration.

G

Ghost Wall—A "robbed-out" wall from which stones have been removed, leaving a filled robber trench.

Glaçis—A "glass-like" slope of beaten earth, often covered with lime, outside the fortifications.

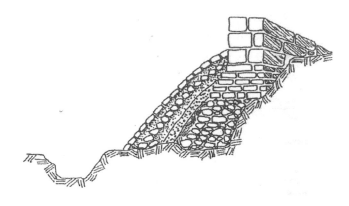

Graffito(i)—Figures of inscriptions informally scratched or painted onto a surface.

Grid—The general surveying organization of a site, based on a grid with the lines oriented to true north, that divides the site into 6-meter squares. The north-south gridlines are identified by number, and the east-west gridlines are identified by letter. Each square is identified by the crossing gridlines in the southwest corner of the square (e.g., 5D).

Gufah—A soft-sided bucket made from recycled truck tires; used for carrying excavated dirt.

H

Hammer-Dressed—Roughly-smoothed building stone, not polished, but clearly worked in antiquity.

Handpick—See *Patiche*.

Header—A wall stone, the longitudinal axis of which is perpendicular to the line of the wall. In construction, they may be associated with *stretchers*.

Hearth—An open, uncovered cooking pit; often characterized by burnt debris and charred stones.

Hoard—A group of small objects (such as coins) found together.

Hoe—See *Turreah*.

Huwwar—Arabic term for soft, chalky, white or yellowish limestone.

Hygroscopic—The property of some materials, like wood, to absorb water.

Hypocaust—A Roman period heating system, often on baths, which consisted of hot air circulated through a subfloor. The heat radiated through the floor ans into the room.

I

In Phase—The condition wherein all the remains visible in a square or field are part of the same occupational phase.

In Situ—Latin phrase meaning "in location". Finds are *in situ* when they are found in their original location. *In situ* finds have not been removed and then replaced.

Indicator Sherds—See *Diagnostic Sherds*.

Installation—A man-made feature within a square that either sits on a *Locus* (e.g., a ring of stones defining a fire pit) or penetrates multiple *Loci* (e.g., a buried storage jar).

J

Jar—A ceramic storage vessel whose opening is half (or less) the diameter of the vessel's body diameter.

K

Kiln—A special industrial oven which was used for baking ("firing") pottery or reducing lime from limestone for the making of plaster.

Kokh(im)—Hebrew term for a *locolus*.

Krater—A large bowl often with handles.

L

Lapidary Script—The writing style on a stone monument.

112

Lapis Lazuli—A gemstone of intense blue color.

Large Pick—A large, hand-held (usually with both hands) primary excavation tool used for loosening large quantities of debris quickly. It is only used when it has been clearly established that an earth layer is devoid of artifacts and thick enough that artifacts lying beneath the layer will not be destroyed by aggressive digging.

Layer—A distinctive earth deposit characterized by and distinguished from other layers by color, texture, consistency and content; also called "soil *Locus*" see *Locus*).

Lens—A verbal descriptr for a small earth *layer* that thins (*lenses*) out and disappears. It is usually considered a part of a *layer*.

Level—The measurement of the altitude of a feature in meters and centimeters above or below sea level; it is obtained by measuring the relative difference from bench marks established by surveyors.

Lime—Crushed limestone with particles seldom larger than grains of sand, and not cemented into plaster.

Lintel—In architecture, the horizontal piece over doorways.

Luculus(i)—A burial niche in a tomb; cf. Hebrew *kohkim*.

Locus (plural *Loci*)—The basic unit for recording features in a square. A *Locus* is any feature, whether man-made or natural, that can be isolated, defined, and related to other *Loci* (or features). At Tall el-Hammam, we have six types of *Loci*: (1) soil *Locus*; (2) wall *Locus*; (3) floor/surface *Locus*; (4) installation *Locus*; (5) burial *Locus*; and (6) skeleton *Locus*.

Locus Number—An arbitrary Arabic number that uniquely identifies a *Locus* within the context of a square. *Locus numbers* are usually assigned sequentially within a square.

Locus Sheet—A form, completed by hand in the field, which records the descriptive data of each *Locus* in the numeric sequence in which the *Loci* are identified.

Locus Summaries—Inclusive data summaries, usually produced on a computer from the *Locus sheets*, that provide complete cross-referencing of the *Loci* data.

M

Main Balk—See *balk*.

Massebah—Hebrew term for a standing stone. Often associated with cultic activity.

Megalith—A single, large stone. Walls and buildings made from megaliths are called megalithic.

Menhir—A single, upright (set on end) megalith, apparently for commemorative purposes.

Meter Stick—A ruled rod, usually one meter long, divided into 10 bands alternating red and white in color and each 10 cm long, and used for providing a definition of scale in photographs.

Microlith—A very small flint tool typical of the Epipaleolithic period.

Midden—A refuse of garbage heap.

Monolith—A single, large, hewn stone.

Mosaic—A floor or wall design made of small cubed stones (*tesserae*).

N

Naos—The central chamber of a temple.

Nari—Very soft limestone which breaks up easily, pieces of which can sometimes be broken off with the bare hand; often described as "decayed" limestone. Crushed *nari* is the easiest limestone surface to make and maintain. It is therefore frequently encountered, especiallt in thin, laminated surfaces which represent repairs made to the original surface. Crushed *nari* can have many particle sizes in its texture, including pebble-sized grains.

Nave—The central portion of a basilica-type building.

Necropolis—A cemetery; literally, a "dead city."

O

Object—Artifacts with possible museum interest; handled differently than other *artifacts*. They are registered with the government, photographed, and drawn.

Object Registrar—Specialist who controls and operates the object registration process by registering each object with the government, describing them in detail on object forms, and conserving them as necessary. The registration numbers assigned by the registrar are entered into the Locus sheet.

Orthostat—Usually a large, thinly hewn stone; often used in walls and placed on edge or end.

Ossuary—A small stone box used for secondary burial of human bones; primarily from the Roman period.

Oven—A closed structure used for baking; distinguished from a hearth by being closed.

P

Palaeobotanist—A specialist who studies ancient botanical specimens.

Patiche—A small handpick; used for carefully loosening hard soil so as to avoid damaging artifacts.

Period—A chronological term referring to a cultural horizon. It is sometimes used as a sub-division of an Age, or may refer to a dominant people group (e.g., MB II period; Roman period).

Phase—A distinct stage of habitation or development as determined by excavation. It is normally a sub-division of a *stratum*, but it is also used to designate temporary stratification before a final set of *strata* are assigned.

Pilgrim Flask—A ceramic vessel with a flat, spherical body (like a lentil), usually with one or two handles.

Pithos—A large, ceramic storage container (jar).

Plan—A drawing of a square (or Locus) as viewed from above; also called a *top plan*.

Plaster—Lime that has been cemented into a fairly hard material; it is usually used for coating walls, often in water storage facilities or *cistern*. In such cases, it is rarely more than 2-3 cm thick and seldom less than 0.25 cm thick.

Pollen Sample—An earth sample collected in order to detect the spectrum of plant life by pollen.

Postern—A secret, semi-hidden gate in a city wall; usually one meter or less in width.

Potsherd—See *sherd*.

Pottery Bucket—A properly tagged (see *Pottery Tag*), hard-walled (usually plastic) bucket used for collecting *sherds* at the excavation site and transporting the *sherds* for cleaning, analysis and registration.

Pottery Reading—The process of examining the form and material composition of *sherds* by specialists to determine the chronological placement of the finds.

Pottery Registrar—The staff member who records the results of the *pottery reading* and registers the diagnostic pieces identified for further analysis and possible publication.

Pottery Registration—The process of registering a pottery (or object) find, including: assigning an accession number, permanently marking the accession number on the item, and recording the *provenance* of the item and the chronological placement of the item from the *pottery reading*.

Pottery Tag—A form which is attached to a *pottery bucket* to identify the *square, Locus* and date from which the bucket contents were excavated. (Note that each *Locus* gets its own *pottery bucket*.) contents came.

Pottery Washing—The process of cleaning the individual *sherds* and *artifacts* to remove soil and other foreign materials prior to *pottery reading*. At Tall el-Hammam, pottery items are soaked in water for 24 hours prior to washing. The cleaned items are then allowed to dry for 24 hours before reading.

Probe—A small, exploratory excavation, typically 1 m x 1 m, that is conducted to test the stratigraphy prior to conducting a larger excavation.

Probe Trench—A *probe* that is extended beyond 1 m in one direction (or in opposite directions).

*Provenance (*or *provenience)*—The place of origin; for artifacts, this includes: site, area, field, square and Locus.

Pyxis—Greek term for a small, squat, cylindrical ceramic vessel.

Q

Quern—The lower millstone upon which grain is ground.

Quion-and-Pier (pronounced: coin & peer)—a method of stone wall construction in which undercut field stones (*quoins*) are wedged between vertical *ashlar* pillars (piers). Also called *a-telaio*. The *piers* are often at intervals of 204 m with the intervening spaces filled with unhewn of semi-hewn stones.

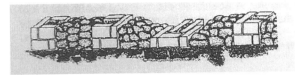

R

Revetment—A wall built below a step of vertical face of a bank (terrace) to prevent slippage or to maintain a level surface.

Robbing—Ancient or unauthorized modern digging into earlier remains.

Roof Tiles—Ceramic roofing materials.

Row—A single line of stones in a wall *course*.

S

Scarab—A seal and/or amulet resembling a dung beetle (*scarab, per se*) which was sacred to ancient Egyptians.

Sealed Locus—A *Locus* which is stratigraphically situated so as to be inherently free from contamination by later or intrusive *Loci*. Usually, this means that it lies beneath an undisturbed *Locus*.

Section—A vertical cut through a *Locus* or *Loci*. The term is also used for drawings of such cuts. A *balk* drawing is an example of a section drawing.

Shard—A broken piece of glass.

Sherd—A broken piece of pottery.

Sieve—The screened tool used for separating objects from dirt. Also, the process of that separation. Sometimes called a "sift" or "sifting".

Significant Sherds—see *Diagnostic Sherds*.

Slip—A thin, outer layer of liquid clay applied to pottery before firing.

Square—A single excavation unit, usually 6 m x 6 m (including *balks*), and is identified by the *grid* designation to which it corresponds. Several *squares* make up a *field*. Excavation of a square is supervised by a Square Supervisor in consultation with a Field Supervisor. The north and east *balks* are integral components of the *square*.

Stela (or *stele*), pl. *stelae*—An upright stone (set on end), often with an inscribed or sculpted surface.

Stratigraphic Context—The scientifically verifiable archaeological setting in which an object, installation, or *Locus* is found.

Stratigraphy—The relationship of *Loci* and *phases* to each other.

Stratum (pl. *strata*)—An occupational level of a site in terms of architecture (contemporaneous buildings) and associated earth layers. It includes three stages of activities: 1) preparation of the site; 2) use of the buildings; and 3) deposition or destruction or abandonment debris.

Stretcher—A wall stone laid so that its long axis follows the line of the wall. In construction, they may alternate with *headers*.

Subsidiary Balk—A *balk* temporarily left standing to clarify the relationship of one *Locus* to another when one of the main *balks* cannot be used.

T

Tabun—The Arabic term for a baking oven; it is usually made of clay and shaped like a beehive; see *Tannur*.

Talus—The debris formed by dry accumulation at or near the bottom of a slope.

Tannur—The Arabic term for an oven which is larger than a *tabun*.

Tall—Jordanian term for an occupational mound (*tell* outside of Jordan; *tel* in Israel).

Temenos—The sacred area of a temple.

Terminus a quo—Latin for "point at which" or the earliest possible date; equivalent to *terminus ante quem*.

Terminus ante quem—Latin for "point before which"; equivalent to *terminus a quo*.

Terminus post quem—Latin for "point after which"; see *terminus ante quem*.

Terra sigillata—A type of Roman pottery covered with a thick red *slip*; often called "Roman red ware".

Terra-cotta—Baked clay, ceramic.

Terre Pisee—French term for *beaten earth* surface.

Tessera(e)—Small, individual stones or ceramic cubes used to make mosaics.

Threshold—The sill under a doorway.

Transit—The surveying instrument used to establish levels.

Trowel—The hand-held, primary excavation tool with a flat, diamond-shaped blade, used to cut or scrape the dirt during removal. In a skilled hand, the trowel can be used to "feel" changes in soil density (*Loci* changes) or artifacts hidden just below the surface.

Tumulus—An ancient grave mound.

Turreah—A large hoe with a squared blade; used for scraping or moving loose dirt.

Typology—The study of the ways in which genres (or types) of objects or features change and develop through time by classifying and sorting them.

U

UD—The casual abbreviation for "undeterminable"; it is used for any object or feature which does not display enough diagnostic characteristic to define it.

V

Votive Deposit—An object or group of objects left in a sacred place. Also called a *favissa*.

APPENDIX C—ENGLISH/ARABIC TERMS

(Arabic terms are spelled phonetically)

General			
All is Well	*kullu tamam*		
Coffee	*quhweh*		
Good	*kuwayis*		
Goodbye	*ma'salama*		
Good Evening	*masa el-kher*	response	*masa en-nur*
Good Morning	*sabah el-kher*	response	*sabah en-nur*
Hello	*marhaban*		
Help	*musada*		
How are you?	*Kif halak*	response	*hamdulillah*
No	*la*		
Please	*min fadlak*		
Tea	*shay*		
Thank you	*shukran*	response	*afwan*
Today	*yom*		
Toilet/Bathroom	*hammam*		
Tomorrow	*bukra*		
Water	*mayyeh*		
Welcome	*mar haban*		
Welcome (formal)	*as-salaamu Aalaykum*	response	*wa Aalaykum as-salaam*
Yes	*na'am*		

Staff			
Archaeologist	*alim athar*	Land Owner	*saheb el-ard*
Architect	*muhandis*	Photographer	*musawwir*
Director	*mudir*	Supervisor	*mushref or mas-ul*
Driver	*shofer*		

Excavation Items & Terms

Altar	*madhbah*	Sherd	*keser fukhar*
Area	*manteqa*	Skeleton	*haikal*
Ash	*ramad*	Soil	*trab*
Bead	*kharazeh*	Stone	*hegara*
Bone	*adim*	Street	*sharea*
Bowl	*sahin*	String	*khet*
		Table	*tawleh*
Bracelet	*sewarah*	Tape Measure	*lata*
Break (rest)	*estraha*	Temple	*ma'bad*
Bucket (tire)	*guffah*	Tomb	*qabir*
Burial	*qaber*	Tower	*borj*
Chair	*kursi*	Trowel	*mastareen*
Cistern	*bir*	Wall	*jedar* or *het*
Coin	*'imleh*	Wheelbarrow	*arabaya*
Dig	*hafer*	Writing	*kitabeh*
Door	*bab*		
Dust Pan	*mankul*		
Earring	*halaq*		
Flint	*suwwan*		
Floor	*ard*		
Gate	*bawabe*		
Glass	*qazaz*		
Hoe	*turreah*		
House	*bet*		
Iron	*hadid*		
Jar	*jarrah*		
Jug	*ibriq*		
Ladder	*sillam*		
Lamp	*sraj*		
Layer	*tabqa*		
Level	*mostwa*		
Lunch	*ghada*		
Mudbrick	*tub teene*		
Oven	*tabun*		
Palace	*qasir*		
Period (era)	*fatra*		
Plaster	*qusarah*		
Ring	*khatem*		
Seal	*khitim*		
Shell	*sadaf*		

APPENDIX D—References and Recommended Reading

Adams, R.B., ed.
  2008 *Jordan: An Archaeological Reader*. London: Equinox Publishing Ltd.

Aljarrah, H.
  tbp This most-thorough study of the Ar-Rawda Dolmen Field is yet to be published (tbp). The information has been provided by Mr. Aljarrah to the authors of this report for inclusion in the Tall el-Hammam database.

Avner, U. and I. Carmi
  2001 Settlement Patterns in the Southern Levant Deserts during the 6th-3rd Millennia BC, a Revision based on C14 Dating. *Radiocarbon* 43: 1203-1216.

Ben Tor, A.
  1992 The Early Bronze Age. In A. Ben Tor (ed.), *The Archaeology of Ancient Israel*. New Haven: Yale University Press.

Brown, R.M.
  1991 Ceramics from the Kerak Plateau. In J.M. Miller (ed.), *Archaeological Survey of the Kerak Plateau*, 169-279. Atlanta: Scholars Press/American Schools of Oriental Research.

Burke, A.A.
  2008 *"Walled up to Heaven": The Evolution of Middle Bronze Age Fortification Strategies in the Levant*. Winona Lake: Eisenbrauns.

Chang-Ho, C. and J.K. Lee
  2002 The Survey in the Regions of 'Iraq al-Amir and Wadi al-Kafrayn, 2000. *Annual of the Department of Antiquities of Jordan* 46: 179-195.

Chesson, M.S. and T. Schaub
  2007 Death and Dying on the Dead Sea Plain: Fifa, Khirbat al Khanazir, and Bab edh-Dhra' Cemeteries. In T.E Levy, P.M Michèle Daviau, RW. Younker, and M. Shaer (eds.), *Crossing Jordan: North American Contributions to the Archaeology of Jordan*, 253-260. London: Equinox Publishing Ltd.

Collins, S.
  2002a A Chronology for the Cities of the Plain. *Biblical Research Bulletin* II.8. Albuquerque: Trinity Southwest University.
  2002b Explorations on the Eastern Jordan Disk. *Biblical Research Bulletin* II.18. Albuquerque: Trinity Southwest University.
  2002c The Geography of the Cities of the Plain. *Biblical Research Bulletin* II:1. Albuquerque: Trinity Southwest University.
  2008 *The Search for Sodom and Gomorrah*. Albuquerque: Trinity Southwest University Press.

Collins, S., G.A. Byers, and M.C. Luddeni
  2006 The Tall el-Hammam Excavation Project, Season Activity Report, Season One: 2005/2006 Probe Excavation and Survey. Filed with the Department of Antiquities of Jordan, 22 January 2006.

Collins, S., G.A. Byers, M.C. Luddeni, and J.W. Moore
  2007 The Tall el-Hammam Excavation Project, Season Activity Report, Season Two: 2006/2007 Excavation and Survey. Filed with the Department of Antiquities of Jordan, 4 February 2007.

Collins, S., A. Abu Dayyeh, A. abu-Shmais, G.A. Byers, K. Hamdan, H. Aljarrah, J. Haroun, M.C. Luddeni; S. McAllister
  2008 The Tall el-Hammam Excavation Project, Season Activity Report, Season Three: 2008 Excavation, Exploration, and Survey. Filed with the Department of Antiquities of Jordan, 13 February 2008.

Collins, S., K. Hamdan, G.A. Byers, J. Haroun, H. Aljarrah, M.C. Luddeni, S. McAllister, Q. Dasouqi, A. abu-Shmais, D. Graves
  2009a The Tall el-Hammam Excavation Project, Season Activity Report, Season Four: 2009 Excavation, Exploration, and Survey. Filed with the Department of Antiquities of Jordan, 27 February 2009.

Collins, S., K. Hamdan, G.A. Byers, S. McAllister, A. abu-Shmais, J. Haroun, M.C. Luddeni, G.K. Massara, H. Aljarrah, Robert Mullins, Q. Dasouqi
  2009b Tall al-Ḥammām: Preliminary Report on Four Seasons of Excavation (2006-2009), *Annual of the Department of Antiquities of Jordan* 53: 385-414.

Collins, S., K. Hamdan, G.A. Byers, J. Haroun, H. Aljarrah, M.C. Luddeni, S. McAllister, Q. Dasouqi, A. abu-Shmais
  2010 The Tall el-Hammam Excavation Project, Season Activity Report, Season Five: 2010 Excavation, Exploration, and Survey. Filed with the Department of Antiquities of Jordan, 31 January 2010.

Collins, S. and H. Aljarrah.
  2011 Tall al-Ḥammām Season Six, 2011: Excavation, Survey, Interpretations and Insights. *Annual of the Department of Antiquities of Jordan* 55: 581-608.

Collins, S. and L.C. Scott.
  2013 *Discovering the City of Sodom.* New York: Howard Books/Simon and Schuster.

Dornemann, R.H.
  1983 *The Archaeology of the Transjordan in the Bronze and Iron Ages.* Milwaukee: Milwaukee Public Museum.
  1990 Preliminary Comments on the Pottery Traditions at Tell Nimrin, Illustrated from the 1989 Season of Excavations. *Annual of the Department of Antiquities of Jordan* 34: 153-181.

Finkelstein, I. and R. Gophna
  1993 Settlement, Demographic and Economic Patterns in the Highlands of Palestine in the Chalcolithic and Early Bronze Periods and the Beginning of Urbanism. *Bulletin of the American Schools of Oriental Research* 289: 1-22.

Falconer, S.E.
   2008 The Middle Bronze Age. In R.B. Adams (ed.), *Jordan: An Archaeological Reader*, 263-280. London: Equinox.

Falconer, S.E., P.L. Fall, and J.E. Jones
   2007 Life at the Foundation of Bronze Age Civilization: Agrarian Villages in the Jordan Valley. In T.E Levy, P.M Michèle Daviau, RW. Younker, and M. Shaer (eds.), *Crossing Jordan: North American Contributions to the Archaeology of Jordan*, 261-268. London: Equinox Publishing Ltd.

Flanagan, J.W., D.W. McCreery, and K.N. Yassine
   1990 First Preliminary Report of the 1989 Tell Nimrin Project. *Annual of the Department of Antiquities of Jordan* 34: 131-152.
   1992 Preliminary Report of the 1990 Excavation at Tell Nimrin. *Annual of the Department of Antiquities of Jordan* 36: 89-111.
   1994 Tell Nimrin: Preliminary Report on the 1993 Season. *Annual of the Department of Antiquities of Jordan* 38: 205-244.
   1996 Tall Nimrin: Preliminary Report on the 1995 Excavation and Geological Survey. *Annual of the Department of Antiquities of Jordan* 40: 271-292.

Glueck, N.
   1945 Exploration in Eastern Palestine, IV.c., Arboth Moab. *Annual of the American Schools of Oriental Research* 25-28 (1945-49).

Greene, J.A. and K. 'Amr
   1992 Deep Sounding on the Lower Terrace of the Amman Citadel: Final Report. *Annual of the Department of Antiquities of Jordan* 36: 116-117.

Harrison, T.
   1997 Shifting Patterns of Settlement in the Highlands of Central Jordan during the Early Bronze Age. *Bulletin of the American Schools of Oriental Research* 306: 1-38.
   2001 Early Bronze Age Social Organization as Reflected in Burial Patterns from the Southern Levant. In S.R. Wolff (ed.), *Studies in the Archaeology of Israel and Neighbouring Lands in Memory of Douglas L. Esse*, 215-236. Chicago: The Oriental Institute of the University of Chicago.

Herr, L.G., L.T. Geraty, O.S. LaBianca, and R.W. Younker
   1991 Madaba Plains Project: The 1989 Excavations at Tell el-'Umeiri and Vicinity. *Annual of the Department of Antiquities of Jordan* 35: 155-180.

Homès-Fredericq, D. and H.J. Franken
   1986 *Pottery and Potters—Past and Present: 7000 Years of Ceramic Art in Jordan.* Ausstellungskataloge der Universität Tübingen, Nr. 20.

Ibrahim, M., K. Yassine and J.A. Sauer
   1988 The East Jordan Valley Survey 1975 (Parts 1 and 2). In K. Yassine (ed.), *The Archaeology of Jordan: Essays and Reports*, 159-207. Amman: Department of Archaeology, University of Jordan.

Joukowshy, Martha

1980 *A Complete Manual of Field Archaeology: Tools and Techniques of Field Work for Archaeologists*. Prentice Hall, 630 pages.

Kemp, B.J.

1983 Old Kingdom, Middle Kingdom and Second Intermediate Period c. 2686-1552 BC. In B.G. Trigger, et al., (eds.), *Ancient Egypt: A Social History*, 71-182. Cambridge: Cambridge University Press.

1991 *Ancient Egypt: Anatomy of a Civilization*. New York: Routledge.

Khouri, R.G.

1988 *The Antiquities of the Jordan Rift Valley*. Amman: Al Kutba.

Leonard, A.

1992 The Jordan Valley Survey, 1953: Some Unpublished Soundings Conducted by James Mellaart. *Annual of the American Schools of Oriental Research* 50. Winona Lake: Eisenbrauns.

Levy, T., P.M. Michèle Daviau, R.W. Younker, M. Shaer, eds.

2007 *Crossing Jordan: North American Contributions to the Archaeology of Jordan*. London: Equinox Publishing Ltd.

MacDonald, B.

2000 *East of the Jordan: Territories and Sites of the Hebrew Scriptures*. Boston: American Schools of Oriental Research.

Mazar, A.

2002 An Early Bronze Age I Public Building and EB II-III Rampart Fortifications in the Beth Shean Valley, Israel. Paper delivered at the 3rd International Conference on the Archaeology of the Ancient Near East, Paris.

McAllister, S.S.

2008 *Middle Bronze Age Fortifications in the Southern Levant: Systems Analysis and Quantitative Survey*. Doctoral dissertation, College of Archaeology and Biblical History, Trinity Southwest University.

Najjar, M.

1992 The Jordan Valley (East Bank) During the Middle Bronze Age in the Light of New Excavations. In M. Zaghloul, K. 'Amr, F. Zayadine, R. Nabeel, and N. Rida Tawfiq, (eds.), *Studies in the History and Archaeology of Jordan IV*, 149-154. Amman: Department of Antiquities of Jordan.

Palumbo, G.

2008 The Early Bronze Age IV. In R.B. Adams (ed.), *Jordan: An Archaeological Reader*, 227-262. London: Equinox.

Parr, P.J.

1968 The Origin of the Rampart Fortifications of Middle Bronze Age Palestine and Syria. *Zeitschrift des deutschen Palästina-Vereins* 84: 18-45.

Philip, G.
  2008 The Early Bronze Age. In R.B. Adams (ed.), *Jordan: An Archaeological Reader*, 161-226. London: Equinox.

Prag, K.
  1974 The Intermediate Early Bronze-Middle Bronze Age: An Interpretation of the Evidence from Transjordan, Syria and Lebanon. *Levant* 6: 69-116.
  1991 Preliminary Report on the Excavations at Tell Iktanu and Tell al-Hammam, Jordan, 1990. *Levant* 23: 55-66.
  1995 The Dead Sea Dolmens: Death and the Landscape. In S. Campbell and A Green (eds.), *The Archaeology of Death in the Ancient Near East*, 75-84. Oxford: Oxbow Monograph 51.
  2007 Water Strategies in the Iktānū Region of Jordan. *Studies in the History and Archaeology of Jordan* IX: 405-412.

Rainey, A.F., and Notley, R.S.
  2006 *The Sacred Bridge*. Jerusalem: Carta.

Rast, W.E. and R.T. Schaub
  1980 Preliminary Report of the 1979 Expedition to the Dead Sea Plain, Jordan. *Bulletin of the American Schools of Oriental Research* 240: 21-63.

Richard, S.L.
  1987 The Early Bronze Age: The Rise and Collapse of Urbanism. *Biblical Archaeologist* 50: 22-43.

Richard, S., and J.C. Long, Jr.
  2007 Khirbet Iskander: A City in Collapse at the End of the Early Bronze Age. In T.E Levy, P.M Michèle Daviau, RW. Younker, and M. Shaer (eds.), *Crossing Jordan: North American Contributions to the Archaeology of Jordan*, 269-276. London: Equinox Publishing Ltd.

Savage, S.H., S.E. Falconer, and T.P. Harrison
  2007 The Early Bronze Age City States of the Southern Levant: Neither Cities or States. In T.E Levy, P.M Michèle Daviau, RW. Younker, and M. Shaer (eds.), *Crossing Jordan: North American Contributions to the Archaeology of Jordan*, 285-297. London: Equinox Publishing Ltd.

Schath, K., S. Collins and H. Aljarrah. "The Excavation of an Undisturbed Demi-Dolmen and Insights from the Ḥammām Megalithic Field, 2011 Season." *Annual of the Department of Antiquities of Jordan* 55 (2011).

Schaub, T.
  1973 An Early Bronze IA-1B Tomb from Bâb edh-Dhrâ. *Bulletin of the American Schools of Oriental Research* 210: 2-19.
  2007 Mud-Brick Town Walls in the EBI-II Southern Levant and their Significance for Understanding the Formation of New Social Institutions. In F. al-Khraysheh, R. Harahsheh, Q. Fakhoury, H. Taher, and S. Khouri, (eds.), *Studies in the History and Archaeology of Jordan IX*, 247-252. Amman: Department of Antiquities of Jordan.

Schaub, T. and M.S. Chesson

2007 Life in the Earliest Walled Towns on the Dead Sea Plain: Bab edh-Dhra' and an-Numayra. In T.E Levy, P.M Michèle Daviau, RW. Younker, and M. Shaer (eds.), *Crossing Jordan: North American Contributions to the Archaeology of Jordan*, 245-252. London: Equinox Publishing Ltd.

Strange, J.

2008 The Late Bronze Age. In R.B. Adams (ed.), *Jordan: An Archaeological Reader*, 281-310. London: Equinox.

Thomson, W.M.

1882 *The Land and the Book: Southern Palestine and Jerusalem*. New York: Harper and Brothers.

Tristram, H.B.

1874 *The Land of Moab Travels and Discoveries on the East Side of the Dead Sea and the Jordan*, 2nd ed. Piscataway, NJ: Gorgias Press LLC.

Warner, D.

2008 *The Archaeology of the Canaanite Cult: An Analysis of Canaanite Temples from the Middle and Late Bronze Age in Palestine*. Saarbrücken: VDM Verlag Dr. Müller Aktiengesellschaft & Co. KG.

Zayadine, F., M. Najjar, and J.A. Greene

1987 Recent Excavations on the Citadel of Amman (Lower Terrace). *Annual of the Department of Antiquities of Jordan* 31: 299-311.

PERSONAL NOTES